ManageFirst®

Restaurant Marketing
Competency Guide

Donated by
◈ Chef Michael Therriat ◈

PEARSON
Prentice Hall

Upper Saddle River, New Jersey 07458

NATIONAL
RESTAURANT
ASSOCIATION
S O L U T I O N S ™

Disclaimer

©2007 The National Restaurant Association Educational Foundation. All rights reserved.

Published by Pearson Prentice Hall, 1 Lake Street, Upper Saddle River, NJ 07458.

The information presented in this publication is provided for informational purposes only and is not intended to provide legal advice or establish standards of reasonable behavior. Customers who develop food safety-related or operational policies and procedures are urged to obtain the advice and guidance of legal counsel. Although National Restaurant Association Solutions, LLC (NRA Solutions) endeavors to include accurate and current information compiled from sources believed to be reliable, NRA Solutions, and its licensor, National Restaurant Association Educational Foundation (NRAEF), distributors, and agents make no representations or warranties as to the accuracy, currency, or completeness of the information. No responsibility is assumed or implied by the NRAEF, NRA Solutions, distributors, or agents for any damage or loss resulting from inaccuracies or omissions or any actions taken or not taken based on the content of this publication.

Requests for permission to use or reproduce material from this book should be directed to:

Copyright Permissions
National Restaurant Association Solutions
175 West Jackson Boulevard, Suite 1500
Chicago, IL 60604-2814
Email: permissions@restaurant.org

ManageFirst® and ManageFirst Professional® are registered trademarks and ManageFirst Program™ and MFP™ are trademarks of the National Restaurant Association Educational Foundation and used under license by National Restaurant Association Solutions, LLC, a wholly owned subsidiary of the National Restaurant Association.

ISBN: 978-0-13-222206-8 (Competency Guide with Examination Answer Sheet)

Printed in the U.S.A.

10 9 8 7 6 5 4 3

Table of Contents

A Message from the National Restaurant Association

Founded in 1919, the National Restaurant Association is the leading business association for the restaurant industry. Together with the National Restaurant Association Educational Foundation (NRAEF) and National Restaurant Association Solutions (NRA Solutions) our goal is to lead America's restaurant industry into a new era of prosperity, prominence, and participation, enhancing the quality of life for all we serve.

As one of the nation's largest private-sector employers, the restaurant, hospitality and foodservice industry is the cornerstone of the American economy, of career-and-employment opportunities, and of local communities. The overall impact of the restaurant industry is astounding. The restaurant industry is expected to add 1.8 million jobs over the next decade, with employment reaching 14.8 million by 2019. At the National Restaurant Association, we are focused on enhancing this position by providing the valuable tools and resources needed to educate our current and future professionals.

For more information on the National Restaurant Association, please visit our Web site at www.restaurant.org.

What is the ManageFirst Program™?

The ManageFirst Program is a management-training certificate program that exemplifies our commitment to developing materials by the industry, for the industry. The program's most powerful strength is that it is based on a set of competencies defined by the restaurant, foodservice, and hospitality industry as critical for success. For more information on the ManageFirst Program, visit www.managefirst.restaurant.org.

ManageFirst Program Components

The ManageFirst Program includes a set of Competency Guides, exams, Instructor Resources, certificates, a credential, and support activities and services. By participating in the program, you are demonstrating your commitment to becoming a highly qualified professional preparing either to begin or to advance your career in the restaurant, hospitality, and foodservice industry.

The Competency Guides cover the range of topics listed in the chart at right.

Competency Guide/Exam Topics

ManageFirst Core Credential Topics

Controlling Foodservice Costs

Hospitality and Restaurant Management

Human Resources Management and Supervision

ServSafe® Food Safety

ManageFirst Elective Topics

Customer Service

Food Production

Inventory and Purchasing

Managerial Accounting

Menu Marketing and Management

Nutrition

Restaurant Marketing

ServSafe Alcohol® Responsible Alcohol Service

Within the guides, you will find the essential content for the topic as defined by industry, as well as learning activities, assessments, case studies, suggested field projects, professional profiles, and testimonials. You can also find an answer sheet or an online exam voucher for a NRA Solutions exam written specifically for each topic. The exam can be administered either online or in a paper and pencil format (see inside front cover for a listing of ISBNs), and it will be proctored. Upon successfully passing the exam, you will be issued a customized certificate from NRA Solutions. The certificate is a lasting recognition of your accomplishment and a signal to the industry that you have mastered the competency covered within the particular topic.

To earn the ManageFirst Professional™ (MFP™) credential, you will be required to pass four core exams and one elective exam (to be chosen from the remaining program topics) and to document your work experience in the restaurant and foodservice industry. Earning the MFP credential is a significant accomplishment.

We applaud you as you either begin or advance your career in the restaurant, hospitality, and foodservice industry. Visit *www.managefirst.restaurant.org* to learn about additional career-building resources offered through the National Restaurant Association, including scholarships for college students enrolled in relevant industry programs.

ManageFirst Program Ordering Information

Review copies or support materials:
FACULTY FIELD SERVICES
Tel: 800.526.0485

Domestic orders and inquiries:
PEARSON CUSTOMER SERVICE
Tel: 800.922.0579
www.prenhall.com

International orders and inquiries:
U.S. EXPORT SALES OFFICE
Pearson Education International Customer Service Group
200 Old Tappan Road
Old Tappan, NJ 07675 USA
Tel: 201.767.5021
Fax: 201.767.5625

For corporate, government and special sales (consultants, corporations, training centers, VARs, and corporate resellers) orders and inquiries:
PEARSON CORPORATE SALES
Tel: 317.428.3411
Fax: 317.428.3343
Email: managefirst@prenhall.com

For additional information regarding other Prentice Hall publications, instructor and student support materials, locating your sales representative and much more, please visit *www.prenhall.com/managefirst.*

Acknowledgements

The National Restaurant Association Solutions is grateful for the significant contributions made to this competency guide by the following individuals.

John A. Gescheidle

James Perry

In addition, we are pleased to thank our many other advisors, subject matter experts, reviewers, and contributors for their time, effort, and dedication to this program.

Teresa Marie Gargano Adamski	John Hart	Terrence Pappas
Ernest Boger	Thomas Kaltenecker	Patricia Plavcan
Robert Bosselman	Ray Kavanaugh	William N. Reynolds
Jerald Chesser	John Kidwell	Rosenthal Group
Cynthia Deale	Carol Kizer	Mokie Steiskal
Fred DeMicco	Holly Ruttan Maloney	Karl Titz
Johnathan Deustch	Cynthia Mayo	Terry Umbreit
John Drysdale	Fred Mayo	David Wightman
Gene Fritz	Patrick Moreo	Deanne Williams
Thomas Hamilton	Robert O'Halloran	Mike Zema
	Brian O'Malley	Renee Zonka

Features of the ManageFirst® Competency Guides

We have designed the ManageFirst competency guides to enhance your ability to learn and retain important information that is critical to this restaurant and foodservice industry function. Here are the key features you will find within this guide.

Beginning Each Guide

Tuning In to You

When you open a ManageFirst competency guide for the first time, you might ask yourself: Why do I need to know about this topic? Every topic of these guides involves key information you will need as you manage a restaurant or foodservice operation. Located in the front of each review guide, "Tuning In to You" is a brief synopsis that illustrates some of the reasons the information contained throughout that particular guide is important to you. It exemplifies real-life scenarios that you will face as a manager and how the concepts in the book will help you in your career.

Professional Profile

This is your opportunity to meet a professional who is currently working in the field associated with a competency guide's topic. This person's story will help you gain insight into the responsibilities related to his or her position, as well as the training and educational history linked to it. You will also see the daily and cumulative impact this position has on an operation, and receive advice from a person who has successfully met the challenges of being a manager.

Beginning Each Chapter

Inside This Chapter

Chapter content is organized under these major headings.

Learning Objectives

Learning objectives identify what you should be able to do after completing each chapter. These objectives are linked to the required tasks a manager must be able to perform in relation to the function discussed in the competency guide.

Test Your Knowledge

Each chapter begins with some True or False questions designed to test your prior knowledge of some of the concepts presented in the chapter. The answers to these questions, as well as the concepts behind them, can be found within the chapter—see the page reference after each question.

Key Terms

These terms are important for thorough understanding of the chapter's content. They are highlighted throughout the chapter, where they are explicitly defined or their meaning is made clear within the paragraphs in which they appear.

Throughout Each Chapter

Exhibits

Exhibits are placed throughout each chapter to visually reinforce the key concepts presented in the text. Types of exhibits include charts, tables, photographs, and illustrations.

Think About It...

These thought-provoking sidebars reveal supportive information about the section they appear beside.

Activities

Apply what you have learned throughout the chapter by completing the various activities in the text. The activities have been designed to give you additional practice and better understanding of the concepts addressed in the learning objectives. Types of activities include case studies, role-plays, and problem solving, among others.

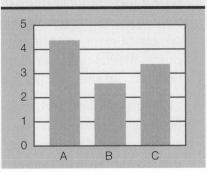

Exhibit

Exhibits are visuals that will help you learn about key concepts.

Think About It...

Consider these supplemental insights as you read through a chapter.

Activity

Activity

Types of activities you will complete include case studies, role-plays, and problem solving, among others.

At the End of Each Chapter

Review Your Learning

These multiple-choice or open- or close-ended questions or problems are designed to test your knowledge of the concepts presented in the chapter. These questions have been aligned with the objectives and should provide you with an opportunity to practice or apply the content that supports these objectives. If you have difficulty answering them, you should review the content further.

At the End of the Guide

Field Project

This real-world project gives you the valuable opportunity to apply many of the concepts you will learn in a competency guide. You will interact with industry practitioners, enhance your knowledge, and research, apply, analyze, evaluate, and report on your findings. It will provide you with an in-depth "reality check" of the policies and practices of this management function.

Tuning In to You

If you wanted to go out to a restaurant for dinner tonight, where would you go? If you stopped even for a moment to think about this question, you have just realized that there are dozens and even hundreds of restaurants to choose from. It is easy to see why a restaurant would want to make sure that your first choice is their operation. As a future restaurant manager, doing the proper research and preparing a proper marketing plan will not only help with your revenue streams, but also help your establishment to stand out from the crowd.

Obviously, restaurants that want to be successful need customers, but how do you get customers? Marketing is the foundation for every successful business, and prospective managers must understand the principals and fundamentals of the marketing cycle. Success in any business involves having a good understanding of who your customers are and what they want. An effective manager will make certain that this is looked at closely and on a regular basis to ensure the success of the establishment.

Additionally, a successful manager understands how to set prices for an operation. Have you ever considered why the same meal might have a huge range in price at two different establishments? You may say that it's not only the meal that you were enjoying, but also the experience of being at the establishment. Pricing is one of the most critical components of marketing, and knowing how to do it effectively and knowing the issues that influence price, will allow you to make educated and strategic decisions in relation to your operation's goals.

Likewise, setting goals for an operation can seem like a simplistic exercise for most. Sure, we want to be successful, but what does being successful really mean? Does it only mean making a huge revenue? Does it mean loyal and happy customers? Or, could it even mean happy employees? Goals need to encompass many layers, yet still relate to the main objectives of the operation. Fully defining what your goals are is an essential ingredient for being a successful manager. In addition to identifying goals, it is also important to adequately plan how to achieve them and track them. The determination of success and of the gap between actuality and goals is critical.

As a result of learning the concepts, principles, and practices described in this guide, you will be a better restaurant or foodservice operation manager or employee. After all, restaurant or foodservice operations are in the business of meeting diners' needs, and marketing is all about determining what those needs are and how to meet them.

Professional Profile

Your opportunity to meet someone working in the field

Robert Gescheidle

Founder
Strategic Foodservice Partners, a Marketing Consulting Firm
Chicago, Illinois

As I entered college, like most college students I had little idea of what I wanted to do. As I pursued a liberal arts degree, I discovered that I liked the business classes best. As a result, I graduated with a BS in Business Administration with a strong dose of liberal arts. In a few of my early jobs, I managed temporary help and even sold coal at one point.

The first notion of what I wanted to do for my career came during college as a busboy and a waiter for the Blackhawk Restaurant in Chicago. It was there I realized how enjoyable it is to interact with people, and that better service reaps greater rewards. Two years out of college, when beginning my career search, I was given three sage pieces of fatherly advice: 1) To best understand marketing, you need to experience sales. 2) Sell what you understand. 3) Work hard and work smart. I followed my father's advice and entered foodservice sales with Nabisco Brands (after all, who can't understand an Oreo cookie?), and it was the beginning of a sales profession that has never ended.

I was a self-starter right from the beginning of my Nabisco career. I studied the product line, and learned how to merchandise and market our products at food shows, on flyers, and in sales meetings. Then I discovered the Nabisco sales bonus plan, and I began selling any Nabisco products that were heavy because the bonus plan was based on pounds. This may not have been the ideal plan for the organization, but it worked fine for me as I sold margarine, coffee, and industrial eggs ahead of Oreo cookies and Ritz crackers. The initiative I took on projects like these led to my being rapidly promoted into the marketing department.

In marketing, I better understood how to sell. (My father was right—sales helped teach me effective marketing and marketing helped teach me effective sales). There is a priority order to features and benefits, and it starts with addressing the customer's needs. This coincidentally gets their attention and delivers value, giving you a better chance to complete the sale.

About now, Nabisco and the Heublein brands (A.1. Sauce and Grey Poupon mustard) were merged. As a result, the Marketing department became overstaffed, so I was transferred to sales management. My family and I were moved twice in this job, first to Florida where I was a region manager, and then to California where I had responsibility for a third of the country. During this time, I learned what it takes to motivate people: start with recognizing what they do right, deliver useful training, and stay out of the way. My teams won numerous sales awards, and I was promoted back into a new marketing role.

Nabisco was evolving during this time. We were customer focused and the time was right to focus on channel marketing (the customer and their needs) in addition to brand marketing. This allowed me (with Fred Paglia) to help introduce Fact Based Selling, a way to quantify and prove our benefits to our operators and the distributors. This connection to the operator's and the distributor's bottom line was witnessed by our ad agency, The Food Group (the largest foodservice agency and now part of WPP), and I was convinced to leave my career at Nabisco and join them.

The Food Group gave me a broader experience by working with many highly recognizable companies and national brands, and I realized that every company does *some* things right. It became my unique opportunity and responsibility to help our clients see other ways to execute marketing and sales in addition to what they are already doing right.

I always had the desire to work for myself and an opportunity came with the Venuso Foodservice agency; I eventually became Patricia Venuso's partner in her small but stable business. When I joined with her, we added Sara Lee as a client and became a very viable agency. Sadly, Patricia passed away and I started a new agency, Strategic Foodservice Partners. The world of entrepreneurship was thrust upon me. My initial focus was getting a Small Business Administration loan, and then keeping customers and employees. There are many details that an entrepreneur must handle that are almost unimaginable in their quantity and minutia. These details do not allow you the luxury of focusing on just doing a few things well, you must do everything well; and you have a lot of learning to do.

We started small with big clients like Starbucks, ConAgra Refrigerated Meats, and Dean Foods. Our competitive point of difference became clearly finding and demonstrating our customers' points of difference. Channel knowledge and effective research became a formula for a clear understanding of their value propositions. As we helped our clients reposition themselves for growth, we were passed up for bigger, full-service agencies. At this crossroads of becoming an agency or a consultancy, a friend came back into my business life, and helped determine the next course.

Our mutual goal was to build a business that would sustain everyone in it, while allowing us to do the work we enjoyed. In order to do so, we needed to build an agency that could reach the size needed to service, sustain, and grow significant clients. We have grown to three offices handling public relations, event management, advertising, promotions, interactive, and total integrated marketing. In addition to a core of small clients, we have successfully added one significant customer each year, including Nestle Waters, Hershey Foods, and the Simplot Food Group. Today we remain in the business of controlled growth, as we continually strive to build unique and sustainable advantages that benefit our clients.

Introduction to Marketing

1

After completing this chapter, you should be able to:

- Define and explain marketing and the major tenets of marketing: marketing concept, the four Ps of marketing, marketing mix, and product life cycle.

- List and explain the major functions of a business in which marketing is involved.

- Explain the role marketing plays in determining products and services.

- List the phases and tasks of the marketing process.

- Describe the ethical and legal issues that face the marketing function.

Test Your Knowledge

1 **True or False:** Marketing is just another name for advertising. *(See p. 3.)*

2 **True or False:** Adopting the marketing concept can change an enterprise. *(See p. 4.)*

3 **True or False:** Customers are the ultimate determiners of product features and price. *(See p. 5.)*

4 **True or False:** The four Ps of marketing are procurement, production, presentation, and performance. *(See p. 8.)*

5 **True or False:** The steps in the marketing process are situation analysis, marketing strategy, marketing mix decision, and implementation and control. *(See p. 11.)*

Key Terms

Bundling	Marketing process
Differentiation	Presentation
Early adopters	*Prix fixe*
Ethics	Product life cycle
Four Ps of marketing	Target market
Marketing	Value proposition
Marketing mix	

Think About It...

In 1776, Adam Smith, the father of modern economics, wrote that the needs of consumers should drive production. This philosophy has only been implemented on a large scale since the 1980s.

Introduction

All restaurant and foodservice establishments should be based on the foundation of excellent customer service. Without customers, the restaurant industry would not be able to meet its goals or be successful. As a manager in the restaurant industry, you must be able to determine who your customers are, what their needs are, and what you can offer that they will value enough to buy. Then, when customers' preferences change, you must detect the change, interpret correctly how it affects your operation, and form a plan to accommodate these changes. Having a solid background in marketing is the first step in accomplishing this.

Marketing is not just knowledge and a set of skills; it is also a *process* that includes identifying what customers want, targeting a specific group, identifying competitors, pricing items correctly, promoting your establishment, and eventually getting a return on your investment. The process of marketing is introduced in this chapter and will be discussed in great detail throughout this guide.

What Is Marketing?

Perceptions of marketing range from a narrow to a broad scope. Some consider marketing to be simply advertising, while others say that marketing is the research done to understand the needs of the consumers. These two tasks are part of marketing, but to fully represent the breadth of the function, the definition must include both the *process* and the *execution* of marketing.

Marketing is the planning and execution of the concept, price, promotion, and distribution of products or services that influence sales and customer buying decisions while satisfying the overall objectives of the restaurant. Marketing includes determining what products and services to offer, how to position them in the marketplace, how to promote them to potential buyers, how to price them so people will buy them, and how to get the goods to these buyers. Within this definition are several levels, which will be covered in detail in the coming chapters.

To effectively market your restaurant or foodservice operation, you should have some basic knowledge about marketing and its tools. This chapter will briefly cover some fundamental marketing terms and the steps of the marketing process.

The Marketing Concept

The intention of marketing is to build a business through an ongoing, cyclical set of activities designed to create, produce, and distribute the products and services that customers need or want. The amount of effort and resources that this takes varies widely, depending mostly on the size of the business. National chain restaurants do a great deal of marketing; independent restaurants do a smaller amount.

In the past, other things drove businesses. For example:

- **Research and development (or technology)**—Managers would ask, "What can we discover or invent that will sell?"

- **Production**—Managers would ask, "What can we produce better or cheaper that will sell?"

- **Sales**—Managers would ask, "What can we sell better or more profitably than others?"

Exhibit 1a

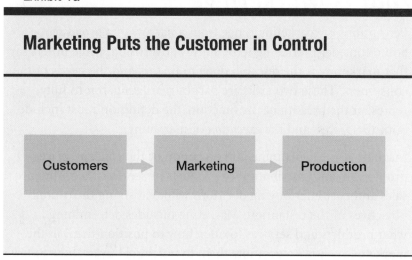

Marketing Puts the Customer in Control

Customers → Marketing → Production

In the current business environment, marketing drives the operation. Managers now ask, "What do people want that we can provide at a profit?" This means that you have to:

- Determine customer needs and wants before doing anything else.

- Determine the costs, prices, and profitability of products and services before initiating production.

- Organize all aspects of the operation to provide what your customers want and not other things.

Another way of saying this is to say that your company is customer focused. (See *Exhibit 1a.*)

The marketing concept puts the marketing function into, and sometimes in charge of, areas of the company and the product development process that used to belong exclusively to other specialties. (See *Exhibit 1b.*) For example:

- The Research and Development department is no longer in charge of inventing what they want; the marketing function now tells them what is needed and what its characteristics should be.

- The Production department is no longer the sole determiner of how to produce the product; the marketing function now puts parameters in place that control costs, locations, and timing of production.

- The Sales department is no longer in control of pricing; the marketing function is now in control.

As a result, a modern marketing function (a department or a person) has four areas of interest and responsibility in the overall process of product development and sales: determining products and their features, determining production parameters, determining distribution, and evaluating products and their acceptance by customers.

Exhibit 1b

The Marketing Concept Changes an Enterprise

Before the marketing concept is adopted...

R&D

Production

Marketing

Sales

Marketing

R&D

Production

Sales

...After the marketing concept is adopted

Marketing Determines the Products and Services

Customers should drive what products and services are created, produced, and distributed. They certainly drive which ones sell. The marketing function determines what products and services customers desire and what the characteristics of those products and services should be.

Determining Product Features and Benefits

The primary role that marketing has in determining products and services is listening to and understanding what the customer wants. The marketing function does this by conducting studies of various kinds to determine what the customer wants; for example, by seeking out their opinions on different products.

In the restaurant business, comment cards and surveys are used frequently to enable customers to provide feedback. This is so important that, to entice customers to complete the comment cards, many restaurants provide giveaways and discounts. (Chapter 2 discusses research methods in more detail.)

Then, the marketing function determines the desired benefits and designs the visible details of the product, such as convenience, speed, form, function, size, weight, color, features, and packaging. For restaurant products and services, it is the responsibility of marketing professionals to determine the taste, quantity, arrangement, type of service, etc. Technical employees like chefs design the internals, such as the ingredients, recipes, and preparation procedures.

Different customers have different tastes when it comes to food, and it is up to the marketing function to determine what those are and define them for the chefs. For example, if your primary customer is a senior citizen, you may want to offer a tasty entrée that does not have a lot of spices or seasoning. As another example, if your restaurant caters to children, you may want to make pancakes in the shape of an animal or shape French fries into a smile and call them "smiley fries," so children will want to return to have more of these items.

Determining Prices

It is known that providing customers with what they want at a fair price will drive sales. But what is a fair price? A fair price is not simply a low price; it depends on the value that customers perceive in what they are buying. (See *Exhibit 1c.*)

For example, a suburban country club has always served salmon on the dinner menu. One day, the chef receives a sample order of Saddle River Salmon from his supplier. The chef decides to test the product by offering the special Saddle River Salmon to a few guests. The feedback is outstandingly high, and the guests who try the new salmon dish thoroughly enjoy it. Customers praise this product so much that the chef decides to permanently carry the special salmon.

However, the Saddle River Salmon is seasonal, the amount available is limited and expensive, and it sells out frequently. The menu manager must determine a menu price that will cover the greater cost of the Saddle River Salmon, but also that is low enough that customers will purchase it, leaving a fair profit for the club. Once the proper price is set, the club's management is happy to see that customers are purchasing the Saddle River Salmon even though it is more expensive than the previous salmon entrée. The product design, production, and pricing are a great success, and more and more guests begin dining at the club in the hope that the Saddle River Salmon is available. (Chapter 4 will discuss the challenge of pricing in more detail.)

Controlling the Production of the Products

Although the marketing function is not responsible for the actual production of products, it is responsible for arranging for the production and those production aspects that affect customers. (See *Exhibit 1d.*) Examples include when an item is produced, how many are produced, and the maximum production cost. For independent restaurants, this is a very small function; it only involves predicting sales, the production needed to meet these sales, and the maximum food cost of each menu item. In a national chain, this function is significantly larger.

Exhibit 1c

Customers communicate an item's value by deciding to purchase the item or not.

Exhibit 1d

Marketing decides when to initiate production and how much to produce.

Determining the Distribution of the Products and Services

The next major task of the marketing function is determining how to make the products and services available to the intended customers. This can include warehousing, shipping, distributors and distribution centers, and sales outlets. For restaurants, the distribution end of the business is primarily the restaurant location. The other aspects come into play primarily for restaurant operations that ship their products directly to the customer. Distribution does not include moving your products from the kitchen to the customer; this is part of your products and services.

Evaluating the Products and Services

Marketing professionals evaluate the success of products and services. They provide the information needed to modify and improve the products and services to be more in line with what customers want. This helps you keep customers satisfied and sales high. You also can issue "new and improved products" to provide customers with an incentive to keep buying.

Over the years, the restaurant industry has altered many products due to customer demand. One example of this is health food, much of which has been changed to reflect the needs and wants of customers. For example, many people today are concerned with high cholesterol. As a result, many cereal manufacturers have reevaluated their products, and now, instead of having low-cholesterol cereal, they provide cereal that can help lower one's cholesterol level.

The Four Ps of Marketing

Marketing has been discussed in this chapter in terms of making product decisions, promotion decisions, pricing decisions, and decisions about placing the product in the marketplace. These are known as the **four Ps of marketing.** (See *Exhibit 1e* on the next page.) The four Ps are also known as the **marketing mix.**

The four Ps are a common way to categorize the different, controllable components of the marketing process and are widely accepted and used on a daily basis by marketing professionals. In fact, many people use the four Ps to define marketing within their establishments. The four Ps comprehensively cover the interests and activities of marketing for organizations of all sizes. Throughout this guide, each of these components will be discussed in greater detail.

Exhibit 1e

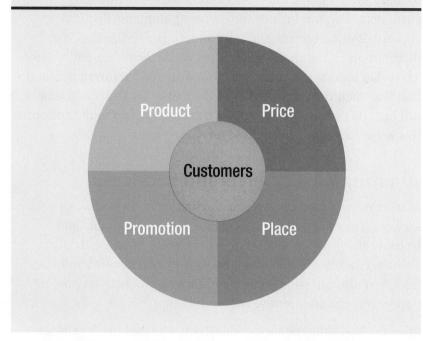

The Four Ps of Marketing

The decisions and activities of marketing can be placed into four categories.

Product Decisions

This "P" category covers decisions about the products (and services) that you want to sell to your guests. Some of the product decisions that a business makes in this category relate to brand name, functionality, appearance, quality, safety, packaging, repairs and support, warranty, accessories, and services. For restaurants, product decisions include the items on the menu, the quality of ingredients used, the quality of preparation, appearance of the items, what ingredients they contain, and policies regarding customers' level of satisfaction with items purchased. It also includes the atmosphere and dining experience that you want to provide.

Packaging is how a product looks when it is on the shelf or has the potential to be purchased. In the restaurant and foodservice industry, packaging includes entrée or dessert displays, arrangement on self-service shelves, and most important, **presentation**—the arrangement of food on the plate. (See *Exhibit 1f.*)

How a product looks affects customers' desire for that product. This is obvious when it comes to children. For example, a dairy company recently targeted its marketing efforts to children and teenagers. They set out to dramatically increase the popularity of drinking milk in these segments simply by changing the milk containers. They designed fun and exciting single-service containers and advertised them that way. Once that happened, children and teenagers thought drinking milk was cool, and the demand for milk increased.

Price Decisions

This "P" category covers decisions about the price charged for the product (or service). The first factor to take into account in pricing is your pricing strategy. The next step is to examine normal retail

Exhibit 1f

The presentation of the food is a marketing decision.

price, wholesale price, volume discounts, cash and early payment discounts, seasonal pricing, price flexibility, price discrimination, financing options, and **bundling**—grouping several products together for one lower price. For restaurant or foodservice operations, pricing typically is limited to the amounts listed on the menu, adjusting the menu price for seasonal tastes and seasonal supplies, and doing bundling such as "meal deals" and *prix fixe* (French for "fixed price") dinners.

Place Decisions

This "P" category covers distributing your product to your customers. In businesses in general, this includes:

- Distribution channels to be used
- Type of market coverage (inclusive, selective, or exclusive distribution)
- Selection of specific channel members
- Inventory management and warehousing of finished goods
- Location and nature of distribution centers
- Order processing
- Transportation of the products to the customers

For restaurant and foodservice operations, place primarily is the establishment itself. However, also included in the place category are decisions about delivery to the customer through catering, home delivery, and shipping services.

Promotion Decisions

This "P" category covers decisions related to communicating information about your products and services to your target customers in such a way that they will buy them; in other words, how you get your message across. How products and services are promoted is a strong determiner of their sales. Factors in the promotion area include promotional strategy, advertising, media types to be used, specific media selection, personal selling, sales force issues such as commissions and quotas, sales promotions, public relations and publicity, and the marketing communications budget. Advertising in restaurant or foodservice operations falls into two categories: major promotions in expensive media like television and magazine (done by national or regional chains) and the less expensive methods used by individual operations, such as newspapers, radio, and coupon books.

The Marketing Process

- Situation assessment

↓

- Marketing strategy

↓

- Marketing mix decisions

↓

- Implementation and control

The Marketing Process

The marketing work previously described covers a lot of ground and is very important to the sales of your operation's products and services, and to the overall success of your operation. It is much too important to be done haphazardly, so over the years, marketing professionals have developed an organized process for doing this work: the **marketing process,** which is depicted in *Exhibit 1g.*

Situation Assessment

This first step of the marketing process involves comprehensive research into the marketplace and customers to be served. Its goal is to uncover needs and wants of these customers that your operation can satisfy in a competitive way. To do this, you must analyze the external aspects of your business situation (customers and competitors) as well as the internal aspects of the situation (your operation's capabilities). Your analysis should cover present and future capabilities. If there is any history of the situation, you should include it so that future trends can be projected. (This step of the marketing process is covered in Chapter 2.)

Marketing Strategy

In this step, you determine how to approach the identified customer needs and wants and how to produce products and services to satisfy them. An important element of the marketing strategy is the selection of the **target market** or markets—those people you intend to pursue as customers.

Another important element of your strategy is your **value proposition** to each target market—an unambiguous description of the benefits the target market will receive by purchasing your products and services. This helps focus all your marketing efforts. (Marketing strategy is discussed in more detail in Chapter 3.)

Marketing Mix Decisions

Once you have the big picture and goals, you are ready in the third step of the marketing process to make detailed decisions about your marketing mix. You will formulate short-term decisions and a marketing plan. (The marketing plan is discussed in Chapter 3, pricing in Chapter 4, and promotions in Chapter 5.)

Implementation and Control

To be successful in marketing your establishment or your products and services, you have to do more than just make decisions and plans. You must also ensure that those plans are implemented correctly and have the anticipated effect. In addition, since the world is always changing, you have to adjust or revise your plans as they are being implemented. This means that you have to:

■ Monitor execution and make changes to your promotions and, perhaps, your products and services.

■ Monitor results and make better plans next time.

■ Evaluate successes and failures.

(These topics are discussed in Chapter 6.)

Exhibit 1h

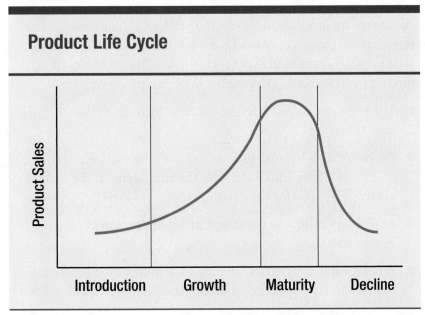

Product Life Cycle

Product Sales

Introduction   Growth   Maturity   Decline

Product Life Cycle

As companies and marketing professionals go about using the marketing process and the four Ps of marketing, they have to do so in the context of the **product life cycle**—the progression all products make through the different phases of popularity and sales. (See *Exhibit 1h.*) There are four phases in a product's life: introduction, growth, maturity, and decline.

Consider videocassette recorders (VCRs) as a recent example of the product life cycle. When first introduced, they were expensive and unknown, so sales were low. People did not have much information about them or understand why they should buy one. Eventually, advertising and word of mouth informed increasing numbers of people, and increasing numbers of VCRs were sold. Eventually, most people who wanted a VCR had one, and sales were limited to replacement units and people buying multiple VCRs. Also, new technology eventually came along in the form of DVDs and DVD players, and sales of VCRs slowly declined. Currently, VCRs are still sold, but in vastly fewer numbers than when they were at their peak. It is expected that they will eventually disappear from the market.

An example of this in a restaurant or foodservice operation is low-fat, low-carbohydrate cuisine. It was introduced and sales increased. Then, sales peaked and declined as people realized that it was not as important to them as they originally thought. Sales now are much lower but still present.

The product life cycle occurs for all products; however, the length of the cycle can vary greatly. Understanding where your products and services are in their life cycles is necessary because the different phases require different marketing strategies and mixes. By understanding the product life cycle and the marketing actions appropriate for each phase, you will better understand how to market your products and services as they go through this progression.

Introduction Phase

When a product is first made available, sales start and grow slowly; customers are just learning about the product and its benefits. In the introduction phase, companies use a lot of promotion to increase awareness, so promotion expenses are high. Characteristics of products and marketing during the initiation phase are:

- There are one or just a few products, which are similar to each other.

- Prices are high because production costs are high, and **early adopters**—those who must have the latest item on the market—are willing to pay for the privilege.

- Availability is limited because distribution networks are just being formed.

- Promotion is directed to building awareness of the product. Heavy advertising often is used along with samples and coupons.

An example of a restaurant that introduces a new product is the Saddle River Salmon entrée mentioned on p. 6. At the time of its introduction, the Saddle River Salmon entrée was difficult to obtain, pricey, and not known to very many people. Management had to take steps to overcome these problems.

Growth Phase

In this phase, sales grow rapidly as more customers become aware of the product and its benefits and as its distribution reaches additional markets. Because of the product's popularity, competitors will normally begin making and offering it too. This often causes the beginning of price competition for the product, at which time additional promotion must be done to increase customers' preference for a restaurant or product and increase its market share. Also, there are product improvements and **differentiation**—making changes to a product to distinguish it from those of the competitors. Characteristics of products and marketing during the growth phase are:

- Additional or improved product features, including quality

- Prices slowly being lowered as production increases, production costs decrease, and competition increases

- Distribution becoming more important

- Increased amount of promotion to market the brand and to differentiate the product from the competition

In the Saddle River Salmon entrée example, if there is a way for more Saddle River Salmon to be caught and made available, more restaurants will be able to offer it, more people will be able to buy it, and similar products will be made available. Thus, competition will increase, and the club probably will have to lower its prices and do some promotions for the item.

Maturity Phase

During the maturity phase, product differentiation is completed and sales continue to increase but then decrease as the market becomes saturated. Competition and promotion focuses on gaining market share, the brand, and the lowered prices that competition brings; in other words, for customer loyalty and attracting customers from the competition. The focus of marketing in the maturity phase is:

- More changes and improvements to the product features as businesses try to meet the wants of their customers and differentiate their product from that of the competition. In some products, these changes are just marketing strategies and do not actually add real value to the product.

- More price reductions to respond to general competition and availability.

- More ways to make the product available.

- Promotion to build brand loyalty and to keep and increase the number of customers.

The owners of the country club at this stage will want to maintain their market position while maximizing profit by being as proactive as possible. They also will want to keep Saddle River Salmon on the menu as long as possible, since it is a popular and profitable entrée. It is possible that the managers will even devise a way to ship Saddle River Salmon dinners through the mail to remote customers.

Decline Phase

After a product reaches maturity, and everyone who desired the product has already purchased it, an inevitable downward phase will begin. This also is due to the fact that new products are continually becoming available and customers' tastes are always changing. The business that does the best job of developing brand loyalty for the product will keep a higher share of the declining numbers of customers. Competition causes the prices to fall, and lower production levels cause the costs to rise. Finally, the squeeze between costs and prices continues until profits are insufficient. Then, the product is removed from the market, first by the weaker competitors, but eventually by everyone. During the decline phase, marketing is focused on:

- Reducing costs through obtaining cheaper supplies, simplifying the product, streamlining production, and reducing marketing efforts

- Lowering prices to clear out inventory

- Reducing availability

- Reducing promotions and making them more focused

At this point, the club should try to maintain the Saddle River Salmon entrée by adapting certain variables, such as lowering the price, creating a new promotion, and perhaps only offering it on one day of the week. The club will have to make the decision to either continue or discontinue Saddle River Salmon altogether if there is no hope of selling it at a profit.

Ethics and Legalities of Marketing

Ethics have been a concern of people for thousands of years and are a relevant consideration of the marketing function. **Ethics** are guidelines or principles of good behavior. These guidelines should be supported by a person's moral beliefs and should provide help in implementing them. Specifically within marketing, there are many areas that could be considered potential ethical problems, and there is often a thin line between what is right ethically versus what is right for the operation's benefit. For example:

- A restaurant advertises a product they no longer carry. Is it right that the restaurant continues placing this ad when it no longer sells that product? (This is a restaurant example of the reviled and illegal "bait and switch" sales tactic.) Is it justifiable for the restaurant's management to say that they are getting customers who would not have come in otherwise? Is the restaurant correct in saying that it would cost too much money to replace the current ad?

Exhibit 1i

Key limes are different from ordinary limes. A Key lime pie must use this variety of limes to be correctly labeled.

Think About It…

Do you know of any other forms of "shady" practices that are found in the restaurant or foodservice industry? Who is responsible for doing them?

■ Another restaurant lists "Key lime pie" on its menu, as many do, even though the item offered is made from ordinary limes. Is it acceptable because, as the restaurateur would say, "Everyone knows that we don't really mean that it is made with Key limes," when actually most people do not know this? Is this illegal or merely unethical? There are a number of menu item names that sound like more expensive products. (See *Exhibit 1i.*) Because everyone else uses them, does this mean that it is ethical for you to use them to make a few extra dollars and keep your staff employed?

Many restaurants are now adopting a code of ethics to help define difficult questions of morality. Having this code in writing is a useful reference tool for you when ethical questions arise. Ethics usually spark some type of debate with both sides of the argument having some weight on the issue. By having a code, you can resolve issues of what is acceptable and what is not acceptable. Ethics codes usually focus on:

■ **Employee relations**—Treating coworkers with dignity and respect

■ **Customer service issues**—Treating each guest fairly and with dignity

■ **Honesty**—Not stealing and declaring all server gratuities

■ **Truth in advertising**—Conveying correct portion sizes, nutritional content, product availability, and ingredients

■ **Pricing**—Fair and honest pricing; not taking advantage if there is no competition

■ **Safety**—Ensuring that the food is of the highest quality and providing your employees with a clean and safe environment in which to work

Some of these ethical issues have made their way into laws for consumer protection. For example, there are laws prohibiting:

■ Misleading advertising

■ Unsafe work environments

■ Discrimination

As a manager, you should become familiar with these laws and ethical issues so that your marketing practices are of the highest ethical quality.

Activity

The Four Ps in Practice

Try to determine for yourself the marketing mix of a restaurant product you buy, first for a national chain restaurant, then for an independent restaurant. Select restaurants and products that are as alike as possible so you can compare them.

National Chain Product

1. Select a national chain restaurant and one of its major products.

2. **Product:** Describe the characteristics of the product, including its service component.

3. **Price:** Note the price of the product. Also note the prices of competing chain restaurant products.

4. **Place:** Interview the local restaurant manager to determine if he or she knows why the restaurant is located where it is. Find out who or what department chose the restaurant location and why.

5. **Promotion:** Find out what forms of promotion are used for the product: television ads, radio ads, newspaper ads, coupons, store signs, table cards, etc.

Independent Restaurant Product

1. Select a local independent restaurant and one of its major products.

2. **Product:** Describe the characteristics of the product, including its service component.

3. **Price:** Note the price of the product. Also note the prices of competing independent restaurants products.

4. **Place:** Interview the restaurant manager to determine why the restaurant is located where it is. Find out what factors influenced the decision to choose the restaurant location.

5. **Promotion:** Find out what forms of promotion are used for the product: television ads, radio ads, newspaper ads, coupons, store signs, table cards, etc.

Comparisons and Conclusions

1. **Product:** Compare the characteristics of the two products, including their service components.

2. **Price:** Compare the prices, within types of restaurants and between types.

3. **Place:** Compare the locations of the two restaurants and how the locations were chosen.

4. **Promotion:** Compare the promotion activities of the two restaurants.

5. Draw conclusions about the similarities and differences, and explain them as best you can with the information you have.

Summary

The marketing concept is that customers' wants, needs, and willingness to buy should drive all business decisions. Thus, marketing involves the planning and execution of the concept, price, promotion, and distribution of products or services that have a bearing on sales and influence customer buying decisions. There are marketing aspects in product development, production, distribution, and promotion. The marketing function has grown in modern businesses to address those aspects. These activities are commonly grouped into four categories, called the four Ps of marketing: product, price, place, and promotion. These are also called the marketing mix. The organized process for dealing with the research and the many decisions that must be made in these four categories is called the marketing process, which consists of (1) situation assessment, (2) marketing strategy, (3) marketing mix decisions, and (4) implementation and control.

Review Your Learning

1 Marketing is commonly defined as

A. the pursuit of customers in different markets in such a way that profit is made.

B. the planning and execution of the concept, price, promotion, and distribution of products.

C. the provision of products using customer research, industrial engineering, modern logistics, and personal selling.

D. the advertising and promotion of a company's products through mass media and a variety of incentives, including discounts, coupons, and bundling.

2 That customers' wants, needs, and willingness to buy should drive all business decisions is called the

A. marketing concept.

B. merchandising concept.

C. management concept.

D. manipulative concept.

3 When a company adopts the concept in question 2, it

A. usually improves its sales force's skills.

B. places more ads and runs more promotions.

C. changes who is in charge of product characteristics.

D. can reduce the number of employees.

4 How does marketing play a role in determining products and services?

A. It does not—the products and services are present before marketing occurs.

B. It discovers what customers want to buy.

C. You cannot determine the products and services without marketing.

D. Before you have any products and services, you need to establish a marketing department.

5 The four Ps of marketing are

A. procurement, production, presentation, and performance.

B. product, price, performance, and persuasion.

C. promotion, price, production, and presentation.

D. product, price, place, and promotion.

6 The marketing process can be described as

A. a way of understanding who your customers are and what they want.

B. a way of determining the demographics of your customer.

C. a way to create, produce, distribute, and promote products that customers will buy.

D. a way of determining whether to start a restaurant or not.

7 The steps of the marketing process are

A. market research, product development, production planning and control, distribution, and evaluation.

B. product, price, place, and promotion.

C. situation analysis, marketing strategy, marketing mix decisions, and implementation and control.

D. introduction, growth, maturity, and decline.

8 The progression all products make through the phases of popularity and sales is called the

A. production process.

B. promotion life cycle.

C. popularity progression.

D. product life cycle.

9 All of these practices are unethical *except*

A. misleading advertising.

B. discriminating against people.

C. suggesting expensive food items.

D. misrepresenting portion sizes.

Assessing Your Business Situation

2

After completing this chapter, you should be able to:

- List components of a market environment.
- Describe the steps in the marketing research process.
- Identify sources of marketing data.
- Explain ways to segment a market.
- Name the parts of a SWOT analysis.

Test Your Knowledge

1 **True or False:** Only large companies have the resources to conduct marketing research. *(See p. 27.)*

2 **True or False:** Your market environment includes internal and external factors. *(See p. 22.)*

3 **True or False:** The most effective marketing targets are selected groups of customers. *(See p. 30.)*

4 **True or False:** Marketing research involves a systematic process. *(See p. 24.)*

5 **True or False:** Your marketing plan should be based solely on your customers needs. *(See p. 35.)*

Key Terms

Barriers to success

Causal research

Competitive set

Competitors

Convenience food

Customer loyalty

Customers

Demand

Demographics

Descriptive research

Discretionary income

Exploratory research

Market area

Market environment

Market research

Marketing information system (MkIS)

Marketing intermediaries

Marketing research

Marketing research process

Menu sales analysis

Need

Primary data

Psychographics

Sample

Sample size

Sample unit

Secondary data

Segments

Situation assessment

Suppliers

Supply

SWOT analysis

Trade area

Want

Introduction

As you learned in Chapter 1, the needs of customers should drive every marketing decision for your restaurant. But what do your customers really need, and how do you know if you are providing it? Answering these questions takes a substantial amount of research.

There are many factors that can affect your ability to successfully market your restaurant or foodservice operation. Regardless of whether you are starting a new restaurant or promoting an existing one, these factors should be researched and continuously monitored. Using a systematic process to do this will help ensure that you obtain good information. As part of this process, you will use

Think About It...

"In 1970, Americans spent 34 percent of their food dollars away from home. Today, that figure is about 46 percent."

—Gale Group, 2004

various tools and methods, including a marketing information system, and different sources of data, such as surveys and comment cards. A great deal of your research will focus on learning about your customers and competitors.

Once you have collected information about your customers, competitors, and market, you can assess your business situation. This analysis forms the foundation for your marketing plan, which is covered in Chapter 3. However, one of the most basic concepts that you need to understand before you start your research is that of customer needs.

What Is a Customer Need?

The primary question that drives all marketing is, "What do customers need?" This question is very simple, but answering it is complex. For example, do your customers need a meal, an experience, or a certain ambience? There are entire businesses and fields of study dedicated to answering this question, and they all are based on knowing that, in order to satisfy a customer need, you need to first know what a need is.

A **need** is an emotional or physical requirement that occurs when a person is deprived of something. For example, a person deprived of food will develop a need to eat. Closely related to needs are wants.

A **want** is a need that is shaped by a person's culture and personality. For example, an American college student might want to eat pizza, while a Peruvian college student might want to eat ceviché. Wants are affected by price, personal taste, and disposable income. You *need* to eat daily to live; however, you *want* to eat in a restaurant (you do not need to eat in a restaurant).

Wants create **demand**—the amount of desire for a product. Demand is the first half of the exchange between the customer and the restaurant, and supply is the second half. **Supply** is the willingness and ability of the restaurant to sell a certain quantity of products at a range of prices. The concepts of supply and demand form the cornerstone for all businesses. For example, a restaurant that is in high demand will have many people waiting for tables. Wants help to fuel demand for a restaurant, which in turn keeps the general public interested in the establishment.

Exhibit 2a on the next page illustrates the relationship among needs, wants, and demands. Understanding this basic relationship is the first part of understanding how to market to your customers.

Exhibit 2a

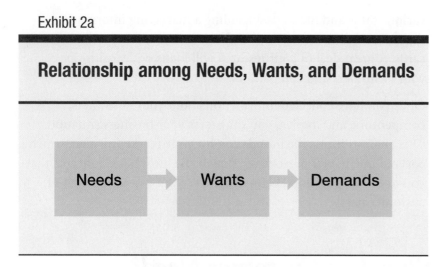

Relationship among Needs, Wants, and Demands

Needs → Wants → Demands

As a restaurant professional, you also should be aware that your establishment is satisfying not only the wants of the public to dine out, but also the need to eat. Therefore, from a restaurant marketing standpoint, there is little distinction between needs and wants. Consequently, this guide uses the term "customer needs" synonymously with "customer wants" unless otherwise noted.

Factors Affecting Your Market Environment

Your customers are only one of the factors affecting your market environment. A **market environment** is the people and forces—both internal and external—that affect a business's success. For example, people in your market environment include your employees, customers, and the general public. Likewise, forces in your market environment include the local economy and local regulations. Because your market environment directly affects your market and the components of this environment can change, you need to understand these components and continuously monitor them. Some of these include:

■ **Physical location**—The physical location of your restaurant is part of your market environment. It includes other businesses and physical barriers, such as rivers and expressways, that can affect your **market area** (also called **trade area**)—the area that your restaurant can serve. For example, a new stadium in your market environment could reduce or increase your market area.

■ **Local economy**—The local economy affects how much money your customers can spend on dining out. For example, the building or closing of a factory in your area may drastically affect the income your customers have to spend on dining out.

■ **Customers**—In discussions on the market environment, **customers** are the people who will come to your restaurant and complete a purchasing transaction. Customers are people who have a need for your establishment and can include those who live in your market area and those who do not. Customers are discussed in more detail in a later section.

- **Suppliers**—Suppliers are the people or organizations that sell the goods and services that a restaurant needs to operate. A typical restaurant would have suppliers for food, linen services, information technology (computers), security services, and other needs.

- **Marketing intermediaries**—Marketing intermediaries are people or organizations that help a restaurant market itself, such as advertising agencies, marketing associations, and marketing research and consulting firms. For example, an advertising agency might help a restaurant mass produce menus to hang on doors.

- **Competitors**—Other establishments that can fulfill your market's needs are your competitors. There are various types of competitors and various ways to assess them. (Competitors are discussed in more detail in a later section.)

To understand the components in your market environment, you must research them.

Activity

Identifying Other Factors That Affect a Market Environment

What other people or factors might affect a market environment for a restaurant? List all that you can think of.

_____

_____

_____

_____

Conducting Research

Just as you would study a map before going to an unfamiliar place, so should you use research data to help make informed decisions. Good data helps you make strategic and wise decisions, while poor data can cause a marketing plan—and the business that follows it—to fail.

When researching information to support your marketing activities, you should be aware of your research options and resources. To ensure that the data you find or produce is valid and can provide a successful foundation for your marketing plan and activities, you should understand the marketing research process and how to apply it.

There are various types of research that can be done to support marketing activities. One is called **market research,** which is information about particular groups of people, or **segments,** in a market. A related but broader type of research is marketing research. According to the American Marketing Association, **marketing research** is information that:

- Identifies and defines marketing opportunities and problems

- Generates, refines, and evaluates marketing actions

- Monitors marketing performance

- Improves understanding of marketing as a process

Marketing Research Process

To ensure that your research data is good, the data should be collected through a systematic approach called the **marketing research process.** As *Exhibit 2b* shows, the marketing research process involves several steps.

Exhibit 2b

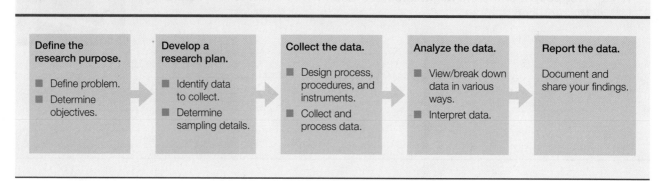

Marketing Research Process

Define the research purpose.	Develop a research plan.	Collect the data.	Analyze the data.	Report the data.
■ Define problem. ■ Determine objectives.	■ Identify data to collect. ■ Determine sampling details.	■ Design process, procedures, and instruments. ■ Collect and process data.	■ View/break down data in various ways. ■ Interpret data.	Document and share your findings.

1. Define the Research Purpose

The first step in the marketing research process is to define what it is that you want to learn from the research. You should define the problems you want to research, and then develop objectives for the research. At this stage, you may have to collect data just to fully define the problem and the research objectives. For example, you might review sales reports to identify day parts, days, or even seasons that you want to research and improve.

Once a problem has been identified, you can define what you want to learn about it by developing objectives for your research.

Depending on the problem, there are three main types of objectives you can use:

■ **Exploratory research** objectives focus on understanding more about a situation and defining it very clearly. The information collected through exploratory research is likely to be used as a foundation for additional research rather than decision making.

■ **Descriptive research** objectives focus on revealing details about a market population. They address the question "Who, what, when, where, and how?"

■ **Causal research** objectives focus on addressing the question "why?" This type of research looks for cause-and-effect relationships.

2. Develop a Research Plan

After you have determined what you want to learn from the research, you can develop a plan for achieving your research objectives. Your plan should describe the data you need to collect. Depending on the type of data you need to collect—primary or secondary—this step can be very involved.

■ **Primary data** is original or "source" data. It is information collected specifically for marketing your restaurant. Typically, it is data that you collect from your own sources, such as customer surveys, comment cards, or interviews, or data that another company collects for you. For example:

  ☐ **Sales data**—Information from your point of sale (POS) system and other sources may be used.

■ **Secondary data** is information collected for reasons other than marketing your restaurant but that is useful for marketing. For example:

  ☐ **Demographic data**—**Demographics** are measurable characteristics of people, such as location, age, income, race, occupation, and gender.

  ☐ **Psychographic data**—**Psychographics** are the psychological variations within a population, such as lifestyles, beliefs, and attitudes.

Both types of data have advantages and disadvantages, as *Exhibit 2c* on the next page shows.

Exhibit 2c

Pros and Cons of Data Types

Data Type	Pros	Cons
Primary	■ Data is relevant to needs. ■ Data is reliable (when the research method is sound).	■ It may be expensive to collect adequate data. ■ It takes time to conduct research.
Secondary	■ It may be less expensive than conducting primary research. ■ Access to data is faster.	■ Data may be out of date, inaccurate, incomplete, or biased. ■ Data may not be relevant to needs.

If you are planning to collect primary data, there are a variety of methods you can use. These include:

- Questionnaires
- Surveys
- Face-to-face interviews
- Observation
- Telephone interviews
- Experiments

If you are using a method that involves some form of interaction with people, such as surveys or interviews, you also determine the following:

- **Sample**—People who represent your target market

- **Sample unit**—Smallest element being researched, such as a business, family, or individual

- **Sample size**—Number of sample units to be researched

3. Collect the Data

After you have a plan for achieving your objectives, it is time to begin collecting data. In this step, you implement your research plan. If your plan includes obtaining secondary data, this is the time to obtain it. For example, you might obtain census or demographic data or hire a research firm.

If you are collecting primary data, you must first develop the process, procedures, and instruments for the research. If using telephone interviews, for instance, you should prepare the interview questions and a form for recording the information. This step also includes processing the data collected. For example, you may need to compile survey results by entering data into a database or spreadsheet.

4. Analyze the Data

Once you have collected and processed the data, you can analyze it. In this step, you look at data in different ways and interpret your findings. For instance, suppose you surveyed both your customers and random people in your market area. You would consider various measures for the customer group, the random group, and the entire group. Also within each group, you should break down the responses by segment. Doing this makes it possible for you to identify patterns based on segment, such as differences between men and women or among age groups.

5. Report on the Data

Your research is not done until you share your findings with others who have a stake in the operation. Reporting your data is an important step because it enables others to review the data and make their own interpretations. It also provides a common knowledge base for making decisions.

The report may be formal or informal, but it is important to document all your findings in a written report. Doing this produces a record of your research, analysis, and interpretation in addition to your sources of data.

Sources of Data

There are many sources of data available to you. You can purchase data, research your own secondary data, or develop your own sources of primary data. The data you are able to collect depends largely on the size of the operation, the resources available to you, and the scope of your market environment.

If you are in a large corporation, for example, you may have the resources to collect large amounts of data and may hold focus groups to learn what people think of a new product. Additionally, you might hire a third-party resource to collect specific data within a certain area through telephone interviews or surveys.

If you are in a small operation, you also can gather data just as large corporations do. Although your smaller company might not have the financial means to conduct extensive research, you can purchase data reports from third parties, distribute your own surveys and comment cards, and research secondary data. There are many free or inexpensive sources for this, as listed in *Exhibit 2d* on the next page.

Exhibit 2d

Market Research Resources

- U.S. Bureau of Labor Statistics
- State and local chambers of commerce
- Professional organizations
- Trade associations
- Small Business Administration
- Private research firms
- Journals and periodicals
- Internet
- U.S. Census
- Libraries
- Directories and guides

Some of the most common methods for collecting data include purchasing or researching statistical records, conducting surveys, collecting suggestion cards, and interviewing customers or potential customers.

Statistical Records

A number of research companies provide data on any number of environments. Competitive research information is available to you to show how one item is selling against another, as is information on current trends or consumer preference for an item. You also may obtain demographic information on a particular geographic area to determine the age group and **discretionary income,** the money left after a person has met all his or her expenses or debts.

While demographic information is a valuable resource for anyone marketing a restaurant, it is only one type of data. At this early stage in the marketing process, basing all of your efforts on one source of data can distort your perception of the total environment.

Surveys

When you want specific information about customers, you can conduct your own research. A common research method used by restaurants is to survey current customers. Sometimes, random people within the market are also surveyed. Using surveys allows you to ask questions about your customers' true needs. For example, a survey might ask, "What would you like to see on the menu?" or "Rate your preference for the following items." To encourage customers to complete the surveys, restaurants often offer customers a free item or discount.

Suggestion Box or Cards

Another common way that restaurants collect their own data is by encouraging customers and employees to recommend new items, services, and other improvements through the use of a suggestion box. Suggestion cards also may be left for the customers with their checks or on their tables. These mechanisms give customers an opportunity to provide feedback to the management. As with surveys, many restaurants provide a discounted or free item to encourage customers to complete and submit their suggestions.

If either of these methods are used, however, keep in mind that the information from suggestion boxes and cards may have a larger degree of error than other data sources. For example, a guest who had a bad day and then received substandard service might react more negatively than he or she would after having a good day. These types of influences can distort the outcome of your research.

Interviews

In some cases, you might conduct interviews with selected or potential customers, or even randomly within the public. This method enables you to have one-on-one discussions with potential customers about their needs. During such interviews, typical questions include asking what items are their favorites, what they typically choose on the menu, and what style of restaurant they typically frequent.

Activity

Finding Sources of Free Data

Search the Internet and the local library to find at least three sources of free demographic data for your city or town.

1 _____

2 _____

3 _____

Marketing Information Systems

To collect and manage marketing data, some organizations, particularly larger ones, use a marketing information system. A **marketing information system (MkIS)** is a combination of tools and procedures for collecting, analyzing, and distributing marketing information that is used for developing, implementing, and evaluating marketing activities. (The abbreviation MkIS is used to distinguish it from another common abbreviation, MIS, which usually means "management information system.") Marketing information systems usually involve computers, databases, reports, and other information resources and can involve external resources and departments.

Marketing research and marketing information systems are not just for large organizations. A smaller operation may also have many methods and resources available for collecting data and developing systems. However, that system may be smaller and less automated. For example, a small operation might use sales reports from a point-of-sale system and handwritten notes from customer interviews.

The two main areas that should be researched are customers and competitors. The needs of your customers should drive every marketing decision made. Therefore, you should fully analyze your customers to make sure that all decisions are based on sound information.

Analyzing Your Customers

Knowledge is power when it comes to developing a target market. Understanding who your customers are and why they spend money at your operation is critical. Understanding the target market enables you to provide the products and services that are needed. It also enables you to direct marketing resources toward the people who buy your products. Having this knowledge is important whether you are just starting a new restaurant, changing a restaurant concept, or marketing your existing restaurant. The more you know about your customers, the better you will be able to meet their needs.

There are certain questions that must be answered when beginning to develop a target market. First, who is patronizing your restaurant? Once this question is answered, you can investigate why customers come into the restaurant. Once these two things are determined, you can research what customers like or dislike about your operation and make improvements.

Who Are Your Customers?

As part of analyzing a market environment, it is necessary to determine who the customers are. You should obtain detailed information about your customers and then begin grouping them into categories, or market segments. Segmentation provides a foundation for identifying a target market because it can help identify the people most likely to patronize the operation.

Exhibit 2e

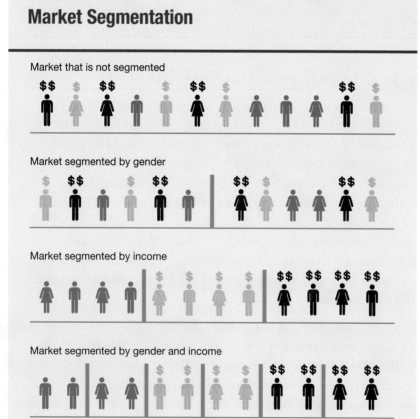

Market Segmentation

Market that is not segmented

Market segmented by gender

Market segmented by income

Market segmented by gender and income

Exhibit 2f

Examples of Demographic Areas

- Age
- Education level
- Ethnicity
- Family life cycle
- Family status
- Gender
- Geography
- Home ownership
- Household size
- Income
- Nationally
- Occupation
- Race
- Religion
- Sexual orientation

There are many ways to segment a market, as *Exhibit 2e* shows. One of the most common ways, and the most critical, is to segment the market based on demographics.

Segmenting by Demographics

Demographics are some of the most frequently used dimensions on which a market is segmented. *Exhibit 2f* lists some demographic areas, and *Exhibit 2g* shows examples of categories within one demographic area, geography. While geography is a critical demographic for local and regional operations (but not national ones), income level and age are two demographic areas that are important to all restaurants.

Age

Do you eat the same things and the same way you ate when you were five? While you may still enjoy some of the same types of food you ate as a child, your culinary preferences and needs no doubt have changed over the years, and they will continue to change as you age. As someone who wants to market a restaurant, you should be familiar with this phenomenon and how it can affect your business; you need to understand the various population trends in aging and the needs of different age groups. *Exhibit 2h* on the next page shows a typical segmentation based on age.

For example, the number of retirees in the United States is expected to drastically rise over the next twenty years, and businesses everywhere

Exhibit 2g

Typical Geographic Categories

Category	Typical Breakdown	Example
Region	■ Northeast ■ Midwest ■ West ■ South	*Northeast:* Maine, Vermont, New Hampshire, Massachusetts, Rhode Island, Connecticut, New York, Pennsylvania, New Jersey, Delaware
City Size	■ First tier ■ Second tier ■ Third tier ■ Fourth tier	*First-tier cities:* New York, Los Angeles, Chicago *Second-tier cities:* Atlanta, San Francisco, Washington, D.C.
Density	■ Urban ■ Suburban ■ Small town ■ Rural	*Suburban (Chicago):* Naperville, Schaumburg, Wilmette, Lake Forest, Oak Park, Orland Park

Exhibit 2h

Typical Age Level Categories

Category	Age
Children	0–9
Youths	10–19
Young adult	20–34
Early middle age	35–49
Late middle age	50–64
Retirees	65 and over

Think About It...

"Over the next forty years, the number of people aged 65 and older is expected to double, while the number of people aged 85 and older is expected to triple."

— SeniorJournal.com, September 22, 2005

are well advised to take notice. In general, this trend is due to the aging of the baby boomer generation (those born between 1946 and 1962) coupled with advancements in healthcare and improvements in the overall quality of life. This demographic group is characterized by a large amount of free time and discretionary income that allows them to frequent restaurants much more than people in the youth, young adult, and the middle-age categories. These characteristics make retirees a particularly desirable market for hospitality, restaurant, and food industries.

The retiree category has unique needs that many establishments are striving to meet. Since health concerns are important to this group, specialized menu selections such as low-calorie, low-sodium, or low-fat items are a huge draw. In addition, portion sizes have been made smaller to suit this category. Even though many retirees may have large amounts of discretionary income, many also need or choose to be frugal with their money, so they seek out establishments that offer low-cost but high-quality meals.

Income

Where customers choose to eat and how often they eat out is greatly affected by their income levels, especially the discretionary income that they have available. Consequently, markets are often segmented according to income level.

Other Ways to Segment a Market

In addition to segmenting a market based on demographics, it is useful to group people by other traits. While the criteria used to segment a market can be virtually limitless, the following two areas are commonly considered:

- **Consumer behavior**—Consumer behavior includes how often people eat out, their spending habits, and their knowledge and attitudes toward a specific product, service, business, or industry.

- **Psychographics**—Most commonly, psychographic segmentation is based on differences in lifestyle, social class, beliefs, attitudes, and other factors. For example, if an establishment is near a large ski resort, it might be useful to segment your market based on whether or not the customers are skiers.

Why Are They Your Customers?

Once a customer base has been identified, it is necessary to find out why they frequent your operation in particular. There are several possibilities.

- **Is your restaurant their destination or merely a convenience?** You should determine whether your customers eat at your restaurant because it is convenient for other activities in their lives or whether eating at your restaurant is the reason why they go out. The results may determine, for example, whether you speed up service or add entertainment for your customers. If your customers come for both reasons, you will have to meet both types of needs.

- **How far do they have to travel to your restaurant?** Determining this will help to determine how far the word about your restaurant is getting. (See *Exhibit 2i*.) If people come a long way to patronize it, customer loyalty is successfully being built. **Customer loyalty** is when customers make frequent, repeat visits to an operation, which shows that marketing efforts are working.

Once these questions are answered, you should find out if you are providing appropriate products and services to customers. Doing this also helps determine whether you should consider increasing your customer base.

To help determine this, obtain answers to these questions.

Exhibit 2i

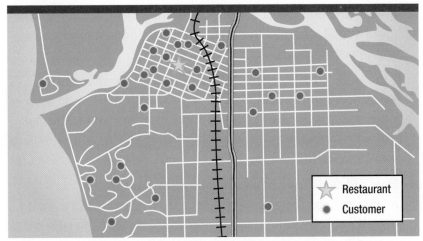

Knowing where your customers come from helps determine how well your marketing efforts are working.

- **Are customers returning?** First of all, are your customers returning? If not, you must ask why, and then take the appropriate action.

- **What is the frequency of their return visits?** If customers are returning to your establishment, you must determine the frequency of their return visits. Is it once a week or once a month? The ideal situation is for your customers to come back night after night with friends, but that is not realistic. A more realistic goal might be to have them come back six times a year. The sooner they come back, the stronger the testament that you are providing the right products and services at the right price.

- **Are they bringing friends?** Are your customers bringing friends or family to your restaurant? Do they think enough of you and your restaurant to invite others? If not, this may be an opportunity to increase customer traffic. If they are not bringing their friends, then you must determine what to change.

■ **What are they ordering?** Determining this can be done through menu sales analysis—counting how many of each menu item was sold, typically by day part and by day, but perhaps also by month or season. This analysis should be done at regular times throughout the day, week, and month. From this analysis, you can tell whether you have a drop off in sales on a particular item, are experiencing a regular cycle in sales, or are involved in an actual upward or downward trend. Your customers "talk" with their wallets. Learn from this, and offer more of what customers want.

■ **Are you receiving compliments from your guests?** First of all, are they tipping well? Overall, customers will reward service staff for an enjoyable experience by giving compliments or tips. If your service staff is being tipped generously, then chances are that your customers are enjoying themselves. If not, then you must figure out why. It is your job to find out what aspect of the service, food, or ambience is affecting this and to make appropriate changes.

Second, do customers give verbal or written compliments? Every operation should make it easy for customers to do so, since comments are a valuable source of information. You can use table cards, the backs of discount coupons, or a questionnaire on your Web site.

■ **How did they find out about your restaurant?** Restaurant managers hope that their customers are giving positive word-of-mouth publicity, since the best marketing comes from customers. If your customers think highly enough of your operation to influence their friends, then customer loyalty is on the right track. Again, table cards, the backs of discount coupons, or a Web site questionnaire can be used to determine how customers heard about your restaurant.

What Do Your Customers Like and Dislike?

As mentioned previously, conducting a menu sales analysis is a way to pinpoint what customers like and dislike about your products. But it will not tell you why they like or dislike certain menu items or services.

If sales of a particular menu item are low, you must find out why. One reason might be that customers are simply afraid to try a particular menu item because they are sensitive to certain food and are unsure about the ingredients of that menu item. The solution may be to identify items that contain potential allergens or ingredients on your menu; this way, your customers can make an informed choice.

Another reason might be that they have an interest in healthy and nutritious food. Many customers today are more in tune with healthy lifestyle habits. Customers may not try certain items if they believe the food is unhealthy. Informing customers what is considered healthy on a menu may influence their menu choices. Before you do this, be sure you and your staff understand government regulations for labeling or calling food items "healthy."

It is rare that customers spontaneously tell you that they really disliked the food or service. And it is even more rare for customers to tell you spontaneously that they liked something. However, they will tell many of their friends afterward.

So how can you find out your customers' likes and dislikes? Ask them. Walk around the room and talk to your customers. (See *Exhibit 2j.*) Ask them probing questions about their experience. If you are sincere in your questions, customers will be more likely to talk to you about their experiences. Asking what customers enjoy will allow you to keep offering those items; asking what they dislike will tell you what to change. This knowledge may assist in modifying the present offerings and identifying new ones. A word of warning, however: voluntary comments tend to be biased toward the negative because happy customers tend not to comment.

Exhibit 2j

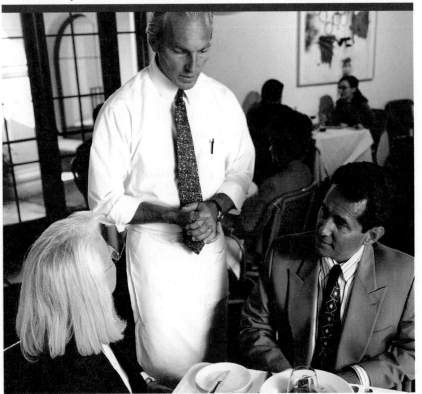

Talk to customers to find out what they like and dislike.

You can use the information you gather to improve your menu and operations. However, you also need to know how you stack up against your competitors.

Analyzing Your Competitors

To be fully successful, a restaurant or foodservice operation must meet the needs of customers better than its competitors do. As part of competing, you should understand who your competitors are and how much of a threat they pose to your business.

There are various ways to identify or categorize competitors. For example, competitors can be categorized based on the threat they pose to a restaurant's market. For example, a restaurant that opens thirty miles from your establishment would be a lower threat than a similar restaurant opening within a mile.

Another way to categorize competitors is by what a restaurant considers to be its competition:

■ **Establishments that sell similar products and services**—For example, a full-service, five-star restaurant would consider other full-service, five-star restaurants their competitors. They would not consider quick-service restaurants to be competitors.

■ **Other establishments that sell similar products but at different service levels**—For example, a quick-service restaurant that specializes in hamburgers would also see full-service family restaurants that sell hamburgers as competitors.

■ **Establishments that sell food, regardless of the products they sell or the service level**—In this instance, the five-star, full-service restaurant would see the quick-service restaurant as a competitor, in addition to family-style restaurants and any other establishment that sells food, such as grocery stores selling prepared meals or **convenience food,** such as premade salads and rotisserie chicken.

The restaurants that you consider your primary group of competitors are known as your **competitive set.** Once you have identified your competitors, research them. Visit these establishments, observe how they operate, and study their menu. Find out what they might have to offer your customers, and learn from it. Also use this information to conduct a SWOT analysis.

Exhibit 2k

Components of a SWOT Analysis

Strengths   Weaknesses

Opportunities   Threats

Conducting a SWOT Analysis

In a **SWOT analysis** (or a **situation assessment**), you identify your restaurant's strengths, weaknesses, opportunities, and threats. (See *Exhibit 2k*.) Doing a SWOT analysis is a simple way for you to understand your current situation and take optimal advantage of the opportunities open to you. Such an analysis is very important to the preparation of your plan and to the success of your operation because it helps you focus on key issues.

Within every part of the marketing process presented in this guide, a SWOT analysis also is a good auditing tool to demonstrate whether a particular plan is working and to gauge the current market environment. (The following information is relatively general; more specific information about evaluating your operation is detailed in Chapter 6.)

Strengths

In this part of the SWOT analysis, you indicate all the strengths of your operation—areas where the operation excels. Examples of strengths include a well-trained staff, a good location, well-kept and clean facilities, strong marketing abilities, high food quality, and service that exceeds customer's expectations.

Weaknesses

In this part of the SWOT analysis, you identify your restaurant's weaknesses. This is done so that weaknesses can later be eliminated or even turned into strengths. Some examples of weaknesses are a boring menu, dirty premises, limited abilities or resources for marketing, undifferentiated products, poor quality products, poor service, high staff turnover, and poor reputation.

In addition to weaknesses, there may be certain **barriers to success**—things outside your restaurant that might cause a weakness. For example, if the products you produce are too difficult or take to long to prepare because of a lack of skilled labor, a high-quality product cannot be prepared for your customers.

Some barriers can be overcome by proper planning and execution. For example, to overcome the lack of skilled labor, you might implement a training program, change your recruiting efforts, or change your recipes.

When you create your marketing plan, which is covered in the next chapter, you will determine how to overcome, eliminate, or neutralize weaknesses and any barriers to success.

Opportunities

This is an area where you as a restaurant manager feel that there could be an opportunity to either increase revenue or decrease costs. Examples of such opportunities include a new business opening in your area, an increased number of tourist attractions, the launch of an independent delivery or take-out service, an ineffective competitor, or a volume discount with a reputable supplier. In your marketing plan, a goal should be to make the maximum use of identifiable opportunities.

Threats

Threats come from outside your restaurant. Identifying possible threats to your business is important so that you can control them before they control you. Examples of possible threats include an increased number of competitors, a price war with a competitor, increased taxes, poor economic conditions, or road construction that disrupts current traffic patterns.

In order to have a successful SWOT analysis, you must be realistic about the strengths and weaknesses of your operation and clearly separate present conditions from where you wish to be in the future. Avoid one-sided subjective statements like, "Good at preparing excellent steaks." Instead, compare your operation to a competitor and state, "Better than our competitors at preparing premium-quality steaks."

Notice that many characteristics may work for or against a restaurant in certain circumstances, such as the location. (See *Exhibit 2l.*) For this reason, it is important to understand that the analysis is subjective and is influenced by the person performing the analysis. Keeping things simple, working problems out in a group setting, and getting input from multiple sources are ways to reduce this type of bias. Once your SWOT analysis has been completed, it is time to prepare a marketing plan for the operation; this is covered in the next chapter.

Exhibit 2l

Possible Characteristics Identified in a SWOT Analysis

Strengths
- Location of the operation
- Good capabilities of management and staff
- Being a new operation that offers a diverse level of service and products
- Quality of your meals and service
- Few or no competitors

Weaknesses
- Location of the operation
- Poor capabilities of management and staff
- Lack of marketing expertise
- Poor quality of meals and service
- Numerous competitors
- Dated operation with a stagnant menu

Opportunities
- Ability to expand your services or menu items
- Newly formed target markets
- Competitors leaving or coming in
- New promotional campaigns
- Technology
- Competitor changing restaurant concept

Threats
- Competitor offering lower prices
- Competitor coming in with new or innovative menu and service
- Negative publicity
- Competitor mimicking a certain aspect of your service or menu
- Competitor changing restaurant concept

Summary

Many factors affect your ability to successfully market your restaurant or foodservice operation. These include internal forces, such as employees and procedures, and external forces, such as customers, competitors, and local economic conditions. To make good marketing decisions, you should learn as much as possible about your market environment, especially your customers and competitors.

Marketing research is a process that can help you do this in a systematic way. The marketing research process involves defining the research purpose, developing a research plan, and collecting, analyzing, and reporting on the data. Part of this process involves using various sources of data. While large operations may have generous resources for marketing research, smaller operations still have access to many sources of data. Some of the most common methods for collecting data include purchasing or researching statistical records, conducting surveys, collecting suggestion cards, and interviewing customers or potential customers. A marketing information system provides tools and procedures for collecting and managing this data.

Two areas that need a lot of research are customers and competitors. The more you know about them, the better your marketing decisions will be. It is imperative to understand who your customers are, why they are your customers, and what they like and dislike about your operation. You also should understand who your competitors are and what threats they pose to your operation.

In addition, the more you know about your own operation, the better you can meet customers' needs, compete in your market, and adapt to changes. A SWOT analysis helps you assess your operation by examining its strengths, weaknesses, opportunities, and threats.

Activity

Conducting a SWOT Analysis for Ray's Best Burgers

Ray's Best Burgers is a large, independently owned quick-service restaurant located in Ray City, a growing suburb in a large metropolitan area. Ray's Best Burgers prides itself on using high-quality ingredients while maintaining the speed of service normally found at a typical quick-service establishment. Customers order their meals at a counter, much like at any quick-service restaurant, and pick up their order, when called.

What differentiates this restaurant from its competition is the quality of ingredients and menu items. For example, its "Best Burger" is made from a quarter pound of premium Angus beef. The sandwich also contains a seven-grain roll, crisp romaine lettuce, guacamole sauce, and aged cheddar cheese. Ray's Best Burgers offers several types of hamburgers, an Italian beef sandwich, a chicken sandwich, three kinds of soup, and several side items, including French fries, cole slaw, onion rings, mixed green salad, three-bean salad, and tortilla chips with salsa. The quality reaches every aspect of the menu, from the homemade clam chowder to the premium French roast coffee.

Ray's Best Burgers has a large staff, almost double that of a regular quick-service establishment. Ray's Best Burgers justifies its higher prices based on its labor costs and food quality. For example, when a customer orders a "Deluxe Burger," it takes two staff members to cook and assemble the sandwich, which normally would take one person at a regular quick-service restaurant.

Ray's Best Burgers is located in an upscale shopping district, and its typical customers are upper-middle class, young adults and early middle-age adults who are single. Marketing research shows that customers choose Ray's for two main reasons: it is convenient to the shopping district, and the food quality and service are perceived as being better than at other quick-service restaurants. Customers also view Ray's Best Burger as a "step up" from chain stores. However, research shows customers would like to see more alternatives to burgers on the menu.

Ray's Best Burgers operation has been very popular so far, but its competitive set and market environment are about to change. A developer has begun building a large office park near the shopping district, which has attracted the attention of the Muy Burger restaurant chain and a few other restaurant chains. So far, only Muy Burger has announced plans to build a store in Ray City. The new store will be located a half mile away from Ray's.

Muy Burger targets young to early middle-age adults, but it focuses primarily on middle-income people. Muy Burger's signature dish is a half-pound bacon cheeseburger. This restaurant also offers several other kinds of burgers, three types of chicken sandwiches, a fish sandwich, and several entrée salads. Its side items include French fries, potato chips, and cole slaw. At Muy Burger, customers order their meal at a counter, and then a staff member brings the order to their table. Food quality is good, but not as good as Ray's Best Burgers. Service at Muy Burger takes a few minutes longer than at Ray's Best Burgers, but Muy Burger is known for its friendly customer service.

Based on this information, what strengths, weaknesses, opportunities, and threats do you see for Ray's Best Burgers?

1 Strengths:

_____

_____

_____

_____

_____

_____

2 Weaknesses:

_____

_____

_____

_____

_____

_____

3 Opportunities:

_____

_____

_____

_____

_____

_____

4 Threats:

_____

_____

_____

_____

_____

_____

Review Your Learning

1 **What is the first step in the marketing research process?**

A. Determine customer needs.

B. Determine the marketing budget.

C. Define the research purpose.

D. Identify the target market.

2 **What is the main task in developing a marketing research plan?**

A. Report on the objectives for the research.

B. Define the problem you want to research.

C. Develop instruments for collecting data.

D. Describe the data you need to collect.

3 **When analyzing data, one reason that it is important to look at the data in different ways is to**

A. help identify patterns.

B. show how data was collected.

C. ensure objectives were met.

D. define the problem.

4 **Which is *not* a method for segmenting a market?**

A. Demographics

B. Psychographics

C. Consumer behavior

D. Market environment

5 **Which does a SWOT analysis involve?**

A. Strengths, weaknesses, opportunities, threats

B. Supplies, workers, occasions, trade areas

C. Suppliers, warehouses, obligations, transportation

D. Surveys, wants, operations, tests

Determining Your Strategy and Tactics

3

After completing this chapter, you should be able to:

- Define marketing strategy and list its components.

- Define target marketing and explain why it is done.

- Define target market and describe the characteristics of a useful target market.

- List and explain four strategies for target marketing.

- Define market positioning and value proposition and explain why they are important.

- List the purpose of and elements in a marketing plan and describe each element.

- Define training gap and explain why it is important when planning employee training.

- Explain the purpose and elements of a feasibility study.

- Define and calculate payback period, payback ratio, and return on investment.

- Explain the importance and elements of an evaluation of the success of your plan.

Test Your Knowledge

1 **True or False:** The development of a restaurant concept is important to the planning process. *(See p. 54.)*

2 **True or False:** A destination restaurant will usually command lower guest checks than a convenience restaurant. *(See pp. 53–54.)*

3 **True or False:** A feasibility study is made before opening a new operation to see how successful it is expected to be. *(See p. 70.)*

4 **True or False:** A marketing plan is developed to increase business. *(See p. 52.)*

5 **True or False:** The evaluation stage in the planning process is to identify your successes and failures based on your objectives. *(See p. 74.)*

Key Terms

American-style service	French-style service	Payback period
Benefits	Gross profit	Payback ratio
Competitive advantage	Margin	Return on investment (ROI)
Convenience restaurant	Market positioning	Restaurant concept
Destination restaurant	Market trends	Russian-style service
English-style service	Marketing objective	Target customers
Fad	Marketing plan	Target margin
Feasibility study	Marketing strategy	Target marketing
Features	Mass marketing	Training gap
Financial objective	Mission statement	Upsell

Introduction

You have completed step one of the marketing process: situation assessment; now you are at step two: developing your marketing strategy. (See *Exhibit 3a.*) Once you have your marketing strategy determined, you can select the tactics to implement your strategy and prepare a plan for doing so. This chapter explains how to do these three tasks.

Your marketing strategy is based on the research you have done about your market opportunities. You have studied the possible customers in your market area and their needs, wants, and

Exhibit 3a

The Marketing Process

Situation assessment

Marketing strategy

Marketing mix decisions

Implementation and control

Exhibit 3b

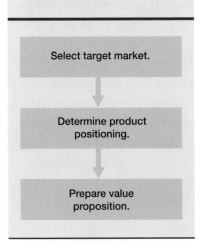

Developing a Marketing Strategy

Select target market.

Determine product positioning.

Prepare value proposition.

willingness to buy. You also have studied your competitors in your market area—competitors of all types, from the obvious ones like other restaurants, to the less obvious ones like grocery stores and home cooking. In this research, you uncovered some opportunities for your operation to address, and you have decided to address them. As part of this research, you also analyzed your strengths and weaknesses. Now you are ready to make some decisions about what to do and how to proceed.

Of course, you could skip the marketing strategy step and just start cooking. But doing this would decrease your chances for success and profit. You are better off starting at a high level and selecting the opportunities and markets you can best address. Then you will know where to focus your time and resources. Otherwise, it is too easy to use them in a less viable niche.

To preserve and communicate your strategic marketing decisions, you should document them in a marketing plan. You can use the marketing plan to share your decisions and plans with others, including investors and employees. There are many elements in a good marketing plan, but you should have little trouble preparing them.

Finally, you should put your marketing plan into action by planning the details of your operation so you can prepare a feasibility plan.

This sounds like a lot of planning for such a simple thing as a restaurant or foodservice operation, but the more effort you put into planning, the greater your chance for success.

Developing Your Marketing Strategy

A **marketing strategy** consists of the major decisions you must make about the segments of a market, which one or ones you can profit by addressing, how to position your products and services in that market, and why that market should buy your products and services. There is a clear series of steps in preparing your marketing strategy as shown in *Exhibit 3b*. Each step will be discussed in this chapter along with substeps and related issues.

In Chapter 2, you learned that no business can be all things to all people; there is too much variety out there. The most effective approach is to break the world into pieces and work on one or a few of the pieces. As you learned, you should identify pieces of the total market: the market segments. Then, you can select your target market or markets.

About Target Markets

You want to select target markets so you can avoid doing mass marketing and instead do target marketing. **Mass marketing** treats everyone in the market as having the same needs and wants. This is good if what you sell truly appeals to everyone the same way; then you can do mass production, mass distribution, and mass communication, and reap the economies of scale that these things provide. Restaurant and foodservice operations, however, deal with peoples tastes for food, drink, and services; these definitely are not the same for everyone.

Target marketing treats people as different from each other and tries to make a focused appeal to a distinct portion of customers called **target customers** or the target market. (See *Exhibit 3c.*) In other words, you should select one or a few of the market segments you have identified as your target markets, and then determine how to serve their unique needs and wants.

For example, you plan to have a restaurant in a major city where there are large numbers of relatively wealthy people with a variety of tastes in dining. You might select wealthy people who like French food and French dining service as your primary target market. A secondary target market might be businesses that want to make a strong impression on their clients. A third target market might be upper middle-income people who want to splurge for a special occasion. Notice that these three target markets are similar in what they might purchase: French food and French dining service. They differ in their reasons for wanting these things and in the frequency with which they purchase them. These differences do not really matter in providing the products and services, but they do matter in promoting the products and services to these different target markets.

Exhibit 3c

Target marketing focuses marketing efforts on one or more market segments.

Exhibit 3d

Narrowing the Field

Potential customers

Customers who can afford your product

Customers to target

Narrowing the Field

The process of selecting a target market can be thought of as a series of decisions that focuses in on markets with potential. (See *Exhibit 3d.*)

1 **Identification of all potential customers in an area**—Those who may have an interest in your products and services; in the previous example, those who like French food and French dining service.

2 **Identification of all customers who can afford your products and services**—The wealthy people, businesses, and splurgers in the previous example. This could broaden if you choose to lower your prices and include less wealthy customers.

3 **Identification of the particular customers you wish to target**—The specific target market or markets you plan to address. In the example, three specific target markets were identified.

To be useful to you, a market segment should be:

■ **Identifiable**—Having differences from other segments that you can measure

■ **Accessible**—Able to receive your marketing communications and to purchase your product

■ **Substantial**—Large enough that winning a reasonable portion of it will bring enough revenue to your operation

■ **Unique**—Having different reactions to your different offerings

■ **Stable**—Enduring long enough without major changes to justify your investment in facilities, equipment, staff, products, and services

Selecting Target Markets

When you select target markets, you must consider two factors: the potential profitability of the target market and your ability to address their needs and wants. In the French food and dining example, you probably could not have targeted people who like French food and French dining service in a small, isolated town because the number of potential customers in this market segment is too small to be profitable. Likewise, you would not want to select people who like French food and French dining service as your target market if you are not capable of preparing French cuisine and providing the French style of dining.

In terms of the market segment's profitability, a segment makes a good target market for you when it has most of the following characteristics:

■ Large enough

■ Steady or growing in numbers, not declining

- Not saturated with competitors

- Not blinded by loyalty to existing competitors

- Able to be attracted with the promotion budget you can expend

- Profitable enough, given the costs you must incur and the revenues you can obtain

In terms of your capability, a market makes a good target market for you when it has most of the following characteristics:

- You have the capability to offer more value than competitors can offer: better food, better drink, or better service.

- Addressing this market fits in with your operation's image or brand identity.

- You have the means to reach the market segment with promotions.

- You have the capital and other resources to enter, serve, and survive in the market segment.

Strategies for Target Marketing

There are several strategies for competing for target markets.

- **Concentrate on one market segment**. This strategy enables you to supply a more limited set of products and services (with the related limited facilities, equipment, and production requirements) and use a limited variety of promotional methods. This strategy is the one usually selected by individual or small chain restaurants having more limited funds. Also, it is the strategy to select when first entering a market. No national chain starts as a national chain; it starts as a single restaurant.

- **Serve multiple markets with the same products and services**. Like the French cuisine and service example, provide the same things to different target markets but use different promotional messages. National restaurant chains use this strategy.

- **Specialize in one thing**. Again, like the French cuisine and service example, provide only these things, not Italian cuisine in addition. In other words, pick one thing and do it very well.

- **Serve one market segment with several products**. Using wealthy people as an example target market, serve more than just French haute cuisine; also serve Russian and Italian cuisine of the very best quality and most fastidious service with extra services such as a sophisticated maître d'hôtel and a professional sommelier.

At this point, you have decided on target markets. Now you are ready to make market positioning decisions.

Positioning Products and Services in the Market

Market positioning refers to how you get your target market to notice your products and services and consider them for purchase. You first simplify the message so harried customers can notice it among the vast number of other messages they are receiving. Then you craft the message to highlight the unique and special qualities of your products and services. (See *Exhibit 3e*.)

A major consideration in market positioning is the power of being first—being the first to market or being the first in market position. Both of these positions are stronger than all other positions. If you are first, you have the advantage. For example, if you are the manager of the country club that first offers Saddle River Salmon, all restaurants that would like to offer it must attack your market position or at least acknowledge and relate to it. If not, they probably will not be considered by their audience. For example, if you are *not* the restaurant first offering Saddle River Salmon, the most popular entrée with your target market, you should not ignore this fact. Rather, you should construct a message that says, "Now that you have tasted Saddle River Salmon, you are ready for Canadian Rocky Salmon (your product). It is the choice of salmon experts the world over."

Exhibit 3e

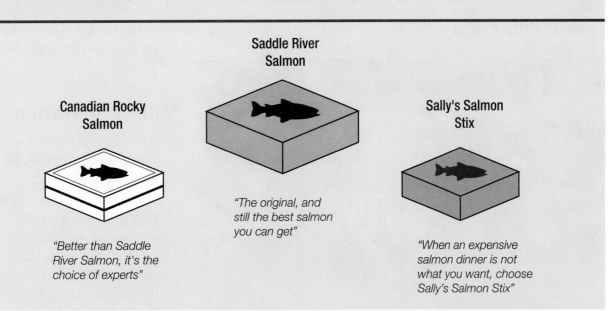

Market Positioning

Saddle River Salmon

Canadian Rocky Salmon

Sally's Salmon Stix

"The original, and still the best salmon you can get"

"Better than Saddle River Salmon, it's the choice of experts"

"When an expensive salmon dinner is not what you want, choose Sally's Salmon Stix"

A product that is very similar to the market-leading Saddle River Salmon must compete directly with it. A product that is different from Saddle River Salmon can position itself independently.

But what if you are in first place? You want to remain there. How can you do this? It would be a mistake to send a message to your target market to remain loyal to your product because you are in first place. This sounds weak. Rather, you should emphasize the qualities that made you first. For example, you might craft a message that says, "Saddle River Salmon—others are just imitations."

If you are not in first place with your product and cannot realistically attack the first-place product, you must use a different tactic. Find your own niche; that is, find an unoccupied position in the field of products that you can fill. Differentiate your product from the competition. There are many ways to differentiate your product: larger, faster, cheaper, higher quality, different features, bundled with something, bundled with better things, time of day, age, location, and convenience, to name a few.

Another market positioning tactic that a non-first-place competitor can use to position the product is to destroy the target market's belief or trust in the leading product. If you are a competitor to the leading Saddle River Salmon restaurant, you could send a message that yours is "all natural, no added chemicals—just pure Saddle River Salmon, oil, and salt."

Yet another tactic is to give your product a better name, especially one that describes its salient qualities. You could compete with Saddle River Salmon by naming yours "Gourmand's Choice Salmon" (implying that yours is a better quality).

Now that you have planned how to position your product in the market, you are ready to prepare a value proposition about it.

Value Proposition

A value proposition is a statement of the value your target customers will experience when they purchase your products and services—how you expect target customers to assess the product and its cost against the benefits they will receive. (See *Exhibit 3f*.) You must specify which target market your value proposition is for,

Exhibit 3f

Value Proposition

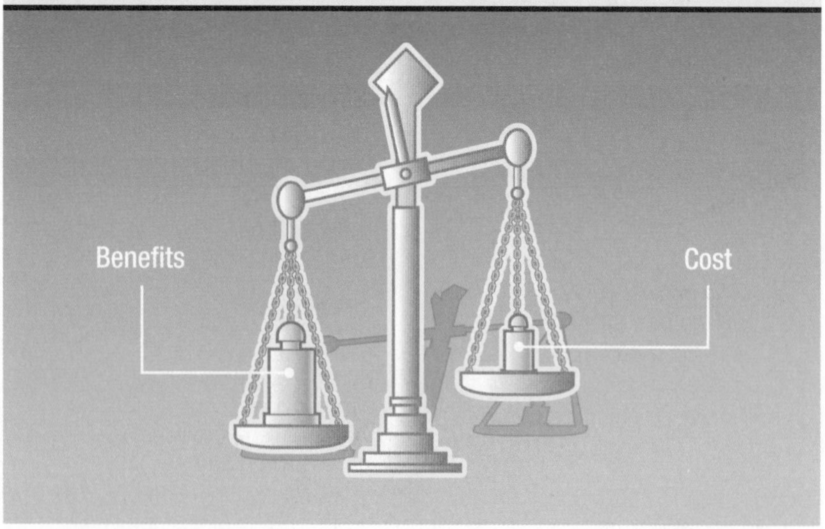

Customers evaluate your product's benefits against its cost.

Think About It…

Opening a restaurant is one of the most risky business ventures that exists. Current research shows that about sixty percent of new restaurants close within three years. What are the reasons for this? One reason may be that the owners entered the business with only a vague idea of what their potential customers wanted and how to provide these products and services.

since each target market values different things. Also, "value" generally means receiving more than was put out to obtain the thing of value. When customers buy your food, they do so because they expect to receive more in benefits than they invested in cash, time, or convenience.

It is important to be clear when talking about value and benefits. For one thing, many people confuse benefits with features. **Features** are the characteristics of your product and its attendant service. For example, your Saddle River Salmon entrée might have the following features:

- Made with real Saddle River salmon, a food not available in the grocery store
- Twelve ounces in size
- Cooked to order on an open flame
- Lightly seasoned
- Accompanied by French-cut green beans sautéed in light oil
- Accompanied by au gratin potatoes
- Served on good dinnerware with silver-plated utensils
- Served at a table with a cloth tablecloth and napkins

In contrast, your target customers are predicted to receive the following **benefits**—something that satisfies customers' needs:

- Wonderful taste sensation
- Effortless dining without having to prepare it themselves
- Pleasurable dining experience
- Pleasant décor
- Courteous waitstaff
- Notoriety of being a trendsetter

The question that the value proposition must answer for your target market is, "Are the benefits worth the cost?" In other words, what benefits does your product provide that your target market considers worth purchasing?

Preparing your value proposition for each target market defines the way you are going to promote your products and services to this market. It lays the foundation for many decisions, activities, and expenses that will be discussed in this and later chapters. However, before you get to those, you should prepare a marketing plan.

Exhibit 3g

Planning can make the difference between success and failure.

Preparing Your Marketing Plan

Planning how to market your restaurant or foodservice operation is the next important step in your marketing effort. (See *Exhibit 3g.*) You will learn why this is true and how to construct an effective, efficient, and affordable marketing plan. You will also learn about doing a feasibility study and a competitive analysis, both part of the marketing planning process.

Of course, you cannot develop a plan without knowing your customers, their likes and dislikes, what they want to buy, and what they are willing to pay. The marketing plan builds on the research and decisions you made in selecting your target market and positioning your products and services.

The Importance of a Marketing Plan

Most people hate to plan. It is hard work that, to some people, is a waste of effort because things never happen the way the planner expected. This part may be true, but that just means that the plan did not have enough breadth or cover enough situations. It is precisely because so many different things can happen and so many things can go wrong that you need a plan.

A **marketing plan** is a document that will help you market your restaurant to increase business. A marketing plan is valuable not only because of the decisions and contingencies that it includes, but also because of the information you collect and the knowledge you acquire during the planning process. That is, the exercise of preparing the plan is valuable in helping you understand how your business will operate in the marketplace.

A marketing plan defines your operation, specifies your goals and objectives, and explains your business to others. A good marketing plan can help you:

- Chart a path for the operation

- Guide the operation to achieve your goals

- Use your resources intelligently so they contribute to the achievement of your goals

- Anticipate possible problems and roadblocks like changes in weather, increases or decreases in customer counts, and changes in customer preferences

- Plan ways to handle the problems and roadblocks

- Prepare your operation for success

However, you cannot simply have a plan in your head; it is too easy for a mental plan to shift as your situation and feelings change. A written document, on the other hand, has several advantages:

- It does not change unintentionally.

- It can be shown to others to gain their support and involvement.

- It can be referenced by others if need be.

- It makes you accountable for executing it.

- It can be a solid basis for a follow-up evaluation of the operation.

One last point: a plan should not merely sit on a shelf and collect dust. It should be shared, reviewed, and updated as situations change in your operation. If you have a plan, you are more likely to be successful because you have already looked at all the elements of your operation and have already thought through how to do things and what to do if things go wrong. In other words, you are prepared.

Elements in a Marketing Plan

As with a SWOT analysis, a good marketing plan has specific areas to be addressed and should answer the following questions:

- What is the condition of the operation now?

- What do we want the operation to be like in the future?

- How do we get from the present to this future?

- How do we know that we got there?

These questions are answered through the marketing plan. The restaurant marketing plan has several parts, which you should determine in the order shown in *Exhibit 3h*.

Type of Operation

Identifying whether your restaurant is a destination restaurant or convenience restaurant is one way to describe your operation. For example, if your restaurant is classified as a **convenience restaurant,** it means that a customer usually eats at your facility because it is convenient for them. An example of this would be restaurants at shopping malls. Customers' primary objective in going to malls is to shop, not to eat. However, if there is a restaurant close by, it may attract the hungry shopper for a meal. Convenience restaurant customers are usually concerned with convenience and speed of service.

The alternative to a convenience restaurant is a **destination restaurant**— one that is a destination of choice for a restaurant customer. Customers who attend these establishments go to them as their primary objective.

Exhibit 3h

Elements of a Marketing Plan

- Type of operation

- Restaurant concept

- Market area

- Market summary

- Target markets

- Market trends

- Market growth

- Competition

- Competitive advantage

- Marketing objectives

- Financial objectives

- Products and services

- Mission statement

- Promotional plans

Customers who are looking for a destination restaurant will have higher expectations and will pay more if those expectations are met.

There are advantages to both convenience restaurants and destination restaurants. Convenience restaurants will have more customers on a given day part due to the ability to turn tables often. The increased number of customers will offset the lower check average that is typical of convenience restaurants. The advantages of a destination restaurant will be a higher guest check per guest and more menu offerings to sell.

Restaurant Concept

Your restaurant concept is the starting point for all your marketing plans. Your **restaurant concept** describes what your restaurant is meant to be: the type of restaurant, the type of customers you want, and the type of cuisine you offer. It states clearly why you are in business and what business you are in.

Suppose you are the manager of Pete's, and you must make many decisions and plans in order to be successful. Throughout the rest of this chapter, you will learn about Pete's Pizza and Pasta as an example.

Market Area

In this section of the marketing plan, you identify the geographic area that your operation serves—the area from which it attracts customers. The people in this geographic area may reside in the area, work in the area, be visiting the area, or be passing through it. Pete's is located in a medium-size college town.

Market Summary

In this section, you describe your existing and potential markets— the people who are in your market area. Some considerations include the number of existing customers, why they are in your market area, a description of your returning customers, and a description of new customers you hope to attract.

You then compare these figures to the market potential. The market potential is determined by studying the geography and the population of the surrounding areas of your restaurant (this will be covered later in this chapter). Specifying the market potential will enable you to identify some realistic measurable goals in the number of new customers and in the number of returning customers.

For example, as the owner of Pete's, you have determined that your existing market is college students, with ages ranging from eighteen to twenty-three. You also understand that two new manufacturing businesses have come to town. You realize that their employees are a potential market you would like to draw into your restaurant.

Exhibit 3i

Your target market is those people you want as customers.

Target Markets

Your target markets (see *Exhibit 3i*) are based upon the type of restaurant and restaurant concept you have selected. Pete's Pizza and Pasta will bring in a certain market that perceives the restaurant as a value—one that provides the desired quality of product and service for the price. You can have more than one target market. Also, you can have different target markets for each day part. For example, Pete's Pizza and Pasta, in addition to targeting college students all day, could target commuters for breakfast, workers in local businesses for lunch, and families for dinner.

Market Trends

Once you have described your target market, you should identify important trends in this market. **Market trends** are long-term increases or decreases in some factor outside your operation, for example an increase or decrease in:

- Population
- Economy
- Competition
- Costs or prices
- Wages
- Popularity of particular products

You must pay attention to those trends that might affect your operation.

Important trends in the Pete's Pizza and Pasta scenario may include:

- An increase in college enrollment
- College graduates moving elsewhere to launch their careers

In order to notice and predict trends, it is vital that you keep up with current events and stay involved in your community.

It is also important to distinguish a trend from a fad. A **fad** is a short-term increase, sometimes quite large, in the popularity of some product or service. In contrast, a trend is a long-term change.

Exhibit 3j

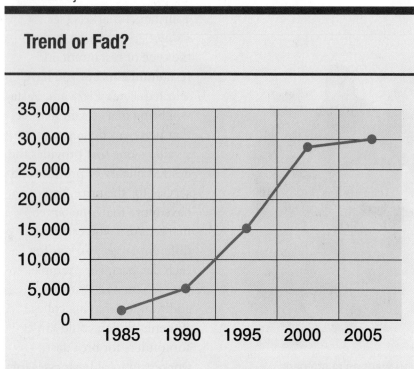

Trend or Fad?

When you first encounter an increase in the popularity of a product, a trend and a fad look similar. (See *Exhibit 3j*.) If there is a difference at this point, it is that a fad increases in popularity more quickly. It is only much later, after the popularity has passed its peak, that you can tell whether you are looking at a trend or a fad.

Market Growth

Once you have determined your target markets, you can determine whether each market is in a growth mode or a decline mode. If a market is in a growth mode, you can aggressively market to this population and try to increase your customer base. If a market is in decline, you may want to target your resources toward another area that has more potential.

In the Pete's Pizza and Pasta scenario, you realize that college enrollment is at an all-time high. More programs are being offered; therefore, more students are coming into your town. You realize that this market is growing fast; however, you still need to consider other markets to develop in case the number of enrollees levels out or if graduates move away.

Competition

Historically, competition was considered to be other restaurants offering similar menu items. Today, though, competition is everywhere. Realistically, competition occurs anytime a potential customer spends money on food other than at your restaurant. Other forms of competition now include grocery stores and other businesses in your area that provide convenience food like premade salads, rotisserie chicken, and ready-to-serve desserts. Basically any food item that is already prepared for the customer can be considered a convenience food.

A major competitor for Pete's Pizza and Pasta may be the college itself since it provides food for its students in dormitory cafeterias and the student union. Other important competitors are the convenience food at the nearby grocery store since it is inexpensive and college students are thrifty.

Competitive Advantage

Your **competitive advantage** is what makes your restaurant different from your competition. Examples of competitive advantages include a convenient location, specialty food, homemade food, personalized service, takeout service, delivery service, ambience, and entertainment.

Some competitive advantages for Pete's Pizza and Pasta could be that it is right across the street from the college's dormitories, and it has free delivery, a frequent diner plan, and a discount for college students.

Marketing Objectives

Marketing objectives are objectives for your marketing plan dealing with number of customers (probably by segment), total revenue, percentage of market to capture, and average check, to name a few. They are based on what you know to be true about your market and your competition. They help you make plans to grow your business. Your marketing objectives should be in writing because written objectives enable you to focus your energies on specific areas of your business. Your marketing objectives should be reasonable (though not easy), measurable, and have a time frame.

A marketing objective for Pete's might be to increase the number of business people dining at lunch by 25 percent over the next year.

Financial Objectives

You are or want to become a restaurant professional because you enjoy serving people along with the possibility of making money. You can provide great food and great service; however, if you do not make money, you will be out of business soon. Attaching **financial objectives**—goals for revenue, expenses, profits, and return on investment—to your plan is absolutely necessary for your plan to be successful. An example of a financial goal for Pete's Pizza and Pasta may be to increase annual sales by $100,000 over the next year.

Identifying financial objectives is such an important topic that a later section discusses it. But first, you have to flesh out your restaurant concept with the actual products and services you will offer.

Products and Services

In the determination of a restaurant concept, you must decide what basic type of operation you will have: quick service, casual dining, or fine dining. This also is the major determiner of the products and services you will offer.

Exhibit 3k

In a quick-service restaurant, customers usually provide a portion of their own service.

Exhibit 3l

In a casual-dining restaurant, employees provide the services.

Quick-Service Operations

The products served in a quick-service operation are limited by what people expect, how quickly the menu items can be prepared, the prices people expect to pay, the time people are willing to spend eating, and the costs of food, equipment, and direct labor. As a result, quick-service operations offer such products as hamburgers, hot dogs, sandwiches, fried chicken, gyros, fried fish, and other quick food. As you can see, these are simple food items with simple preparation requirements, which keep the cost as low as possible.

The services of these operations are limited and, of course, quick; this speed is their primary competitive point of difference. As a result, the service is very limited in nature and portions of it are often provided by the customers for themselves. (See *Exhibit 3k.*) The menu usually is posted on the wall. Customers usually order at one end of a counter and pick up the food at the other end of the counter. The food typically is served in paper or plastic containers. Customers also usually pick up their own utensils and condiments from a central station and then take everything to a table they find for themselves. It is common for customers to clear the table of plates and utensils and place them into trash receptacles. Some quick-service operations provide more table services like bringing the food to the table where the customer is waiting. Overall, the limited services are the least costly to provide of all restaurant types.

Casual-Dining Operations

The products served in a casual-dining operation are more extensive than those of a quick-service restaurant, as are the kitchen equipment and chefs' skills. Although the range of products may be quite extensive, these operations almost always select a category of cuisine, either by nationality or region of cuisine, such as Italian, French, Chinese, or Southern, or by type of entrée, such as steak or pizza. Once this categorization has been made, the choice of products is fairly straightforward. Overall, in comparison to the products of the quick-service operation, the products of the casual-dining operation are more complex and more complicated to prepare; thus, the products are more costly.

The services also are more extensive, and most of the service is done by employees of the operation called servers, service staff, or waitstaff. (See *Exhibit 3l.*) If the operation has a liquor license, there is a bartender to mix the drinks. There is usually a greeter, host, or hostess to welcome the customers, show them to a table, and provide a printed menu. At the table, the server explains any specials of the day and takes beverage orders. Later, the server returns to take the meal order. There may be several courses, such as appetizer, entrée, and dessert; sometimes these are ordered together, but more commonly they are ordered at separate times. The server delivers this order to the kitchen and waits for it to be prepared. The server then delivers the food to the table. There are some differences at this point in how the food is actually served; the options are covered in "Types of Table Service," which follows. During the meal, the server or an assistant fills beverages and checks on the customers' satisfaction level. After each course, a busser picks up the used dishes and utensils and takes them to be washed. After the meal, the server presents the tab to the table and then later collects payment. There may be paper or linen tablecloths and napkins.

All these services cost quite a lot in comparison to the more limited services provided at quick-service operations. Also, the quality of these services and the compensation of employees who provide these services vary markedly over this category of operation, but they are distinctly more costly to provide than those of quick-service restaurants.

Fine-Dining Operations

The products served in a fine-dining operation are usually more limited in variety than in other types of restaurants; food tends to be of Western European countries. This is not to say that there are no fine-dining operations representing other cuisines, only that these are less common in the United States. Regardless of cuisine, only the finest dishes and methods are selected. The kitchen equipment is fairly standard, but the chef's skills are extensive and actually a point of competitive difference. In this type of operation, the products are more complex, are made from the finest ingredients, and are substantially more complicated to prepare. The nature of the food and nonfood supplies is more extensive and more expensive. There usually will be a wine cellar and perhaps a beer and ale cellar as well. As a result, the products are the most costly to produce and, thus, the most expensive of all restaurant types.

The service provided at these operations is similar in type to that provided by casual-dining operations, with a few notable additions. The primary difference lies in the quality of these services and the compensation of employees who provide these services; both the quality and the compensation are much higher in fine-dining operations. (See *Exhibit 3m*.) In fact, it is the difference in quality that makes an operation a fine-dining operation.

There are additional services as well. One typically included is a sommelier who assists customers in selecting wines to go with each course. There also may be additional service providers such as parking valets, coatroom attendants, and restroom attendants. Almost always there will be linen napkins and tablecloths; and usually the utensils

Exhibit 3m

In a fine-dining restaurant, employees provide more extensive and more elaborate services.

will be silver or silver plated. Also, the types and numbers of utensils will be substantially greater with up to a dozen needed for each diner. Again, these services are substantially more extensive than those of a casual-dining operation, and they cost substantially more to provide.

Types of Table Service

In the restaurant industry, there are several different styles of table service that date back for generations. These different styles typically are found only in casual and fine-dining establishments. Each style demands different preparation and presentation procedures. The more labor intensive the style of service, the more costly it is to the restaurant owner to provide. Four styles of table service commonly used in restaurants in the United States are described in *Exhibit 3n*.

Obviously, the types and extent of products and services provided affect many things, and these all must be taken into account when making critical decisions about service:

- Target market you choose and how well your operation can meet its demands

- Size, décor, and cost of the facility, its equipment, and its furnishings

- Number and types of employees, the skills they must have, and the amount of compensation they require

- Types and costs of the food and nonfood supplies

- Extent and nature of your marketing, advertising, and promotions

Basically, the more service provided, the more investment required, and the more ongoing expenses incurred. As a result, more must be charged for the meals because the meals are the primary source of revenue for all the products and services provided.

Mission Statement

A useful addition to the restaurant concept is a **mission statement**—the written purpose of the operation, describing its reason for existence.

Creating this nugget of purpose is a useful tool for all businesses, including restaurant and foodservice operations, because it lets you communicate your operation's purpose easily to investors, customers, and employees. It also helps you remember why you are in the restaurant business and helps you make choices as you plan and manage your business.

Exhibit 3n

Styles of Table Service

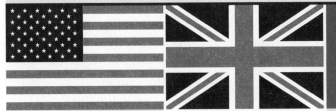

American-style service: The food is placed onto a plate for each diner and then brought out to the customer. The plates are distributed to the proper diners. This is the most common form of table service in the United States.

English-style service: Also known as family-style dining, this type of service is the simplest and least expensive. The food is brought to the tables on platters and serving bowls. The host of the table then serves the meal on the plates for the other diners, or the dishes are passed around the table so diners can serve themselves.

French-style service: While this is the most elegant of the styles of service, it is also the most expensive. The food is placed into serving dishes and then brought out on a cart. It is then served onto the diners' plates at the table. The food is kept hot by a warming unit in each cart. This type of service is expensive to implement because of the expensive carts and the additional skills required of the servers.

Russian-style service: Each diner's hot food is placed onto hot plates and cold food onto cold plates. All the diners' plates are brought to the table on a cart where they are distributed to the diners. A small investment is required by the restaurant owner for the expense of the carts.

Mission Statement Characteristics

To be most useful, mission statements should be:

- **Easy to explain and understand**—Mission statements should focus directly on the goals that the owners envision and should be easily understood by everyone involved.

- **Focused**—The mission statement should be very specific and relatively narrow so that the operation has clear goals to achieve.

- **Straightforward**—The mission statement should be clear, unambiguous, and succinct. It should avoid wordiness because that dilutes the message and confuses the reader. It should get directly to the point of what you want to accomplish.

- **Realistic**—The operation should be able to be meet the commitments.

Exhibit 3o

Mission Statement Topics

Sample Mission Statement

Our mission is to provide only the freshest and finest food and the highest degree of service possible at a reasonable price to our guests. We will treat every guest like cherished family members visiting our home because we realize that, without our customers, our business would not exist. We will strive to keep all areas of our restaurant spotless. We will do everything possible to protect our environment regardless of cost to ourselves. And we will treat all employees with respect and honor their personal needs in every way possible.

Mission statements usually focus on five main points, (see *Exhibit 3o*), though not all mission statements cover all five points. It is the decision of the owners to include or exclude any of these points and the amount of attention to pay to each point.

■ **Customers**—Most service-focused businesses center on the customer. Restaurants usually start their mission statements with mentioning the customer as being the main focus of their commitment to quality and excellent service. The mission statement may use the term "service excellence" or "using the best quality of ingredients available." Depending on the restaurant, it may also include providing the guest with the best possible value and/or providing the guest with an enjoyable eating experience. Basically this section focuses on what the customer should experience from eating in the establishment.

■ **Employees**—Statements that the owners and managers will provide their employees with jobs that are safe, profitable, challenging, and any number of positive job qualities. The mission statement also may include a section that commits to employees that they will be treated with dignity and that the owners will embrace diversity. Within the mission statement, the duties of the employees are discussed, usually including their commitment to the position and their interaction with the general public. This latter statement is often a subpoint within the mission statement. The focus is ultimately the customer, but since the retention of employees is an ever-increasing problem within the industry, owners are now defining this section to include the rights and duties that the restaurant has to its employees.

■ **Shareholders**—Restaurants that are part of a large franchise or chain will usually have a section in their mission statement regarding their commitment to the shareholders of their company. This section will usually include statements concerning the commitment to provide a profitable return on investment for the shareholders. As with all of these sections, the amount of attention given to shareholders within the mission statement is usually an indication of their importance to the overall goals of the restaurant.

■ **Communities**—A mission statement may also include a commitment to communities locally, nationally, or internationally. It might discuss giving back to the community in terms of charitable contributions or being a positive role model for other businesses. It also may discuss a commitment to the environment; for example, ensuring environmentally sound carryout packaging.

■ **Suppliers**—The goal of many restaurants is to provide the best possible meals to their guests, which requires them to be selective in their food suppliers. Reference to the suppliers in the mission statement may include wording such as "providing the freshest possible ingredients to the customers." There also is a recent trend to ensure that suppliers are providing ingredients in an ethical manner.

Promotion Plans

A marketing plan also covers high-level planning and budgeting for all the elements of your promotion efforts, such as:

■ Print advertising in newspapers, local magazines, and flyers

■ Mass media advertising on radio and television and in major periodicals

■ Press releases

■ Internet advertising

■ Press editorial or feature articles

■ Investor presentations and materials

■ Speaking, writing, demonstrating, and teaching opportunities

■ Promotion materials such as brochures or sample menus

Now that you have a marketing plan, there is more planning you should do so you can realize its objectives. You must plan your operating details.

Planning the Operating Details

Operating details should be planned, so you can determine what you have to do and spend to implement your marketing plan. Included are:

■ Determining processes, tasks, and standards

- Determining facilities and equipment

- Determining staffing needs

- Developing staff skills

Then you will be ready to open your doors or offer your new products and services.

Determining Processes, Tasks, and Standards

At this point you have decided what products and services to offer. The next step is to define the processes and standards that are needed to deliver those products and services. Some of the things that must be decided are:

- Menu items to offer

- Recipes to produce these menu items

- Food supplies needed and where to obtain them

- Nonfood supplies needed and where to obtain them

- Tasks that must be done, for example: taking reservations, greeting and seating guests, taking orders, delivering orders to the kitchen and bar, delivering food and beverages to tables, and accepting payment

- Procedures for every task

- Time estimates for every task, as well as the capability of each type of worker for these tasks, such as how many meals per hour a chef can prepare

- Standards for every product and service provided (in addition to recipes), such as standards for plating each menu item and standards for reservation information

Determining these things is the bulk of the planning process, and they are necessary for determining your need for facilities, equipment, and staffing. Writing down processes, procedures, and standards and making them accessible for all managers and employees to use will go a long way toward achieving the goals you have established. (See *Exhibit 3p.*)

Exhibit 3p

Pete's Pizza & Pasta
Policies and Procedures

Written processes, procedures, and standards make implementing the marketing plan more successful.

Determining Facilities and Equipment

The types and extent of cuisine and service determine the facilities and equipment you need. For small, simple products and services, you need only a small, simple kitchen and either a small dining area or none at all. The décor can be utilitarian or have a simple theme; to keep costs down, it might be easy to clean. For more extensive menus and more elaborate services, larger, more elaborate facilities and equipment are needed. There might be special cooking equipment, separate types of preparation areas, extensive storage facilities, and even a wine cellar.

Designing and equipping a restaurant or foodservice operation is a major undertaking, and consultants often are used to help. Entire books and careers are devoted to this area. Since this is a guide about marketing your operation, you may want to consult with other books or resources for more information in this area. Suffice it to say that you must determine the budget for these initial, and sometimes ongoing, expenses. The budget will be used in your feasibility study as part of the cost that must be covered by revenue.

Determining Staffing Needs

Now that you know exactly what you want to do, how you want to do it, and what it should look like when it is done, you are ready to determine what types and numbers of employees you need. (See *Exhibit 3q.*) This is where the previous capacity estimates come in.

Exhibit 3q

People are your most important asset.

This is not a simple matter of dividing the capacities into the planned products and services, although that is part of it. You must allow for inefficiencies and wasted time. Typically, you should plan for each employee to be busy no more than 80 percent of the time at planned duties. The other 20 percent of time will be spent dealing with the unexpected. To handle situations in which you need less than a full-time employee:

- You can hire part-time or shift employees so that they are not paid when they are not needed.

- Sometimes you can assign one person to different types of tasks. For example, the bartender can take the reservations in the middle of the day while setting up for the evening meal.

In addition, you must estimate the skills and knowledge needed for each employee. You will probably have some highly skilled employees, such as a master chef and lead server, some moderately skilled employees, such as ordinary chefs and servers, and some low skilled employees, such as vegetable peelers and dishwashers. You will need the estimates for types, numbers, and skills of employees in order to hire them, and also for estimating overall labor costs.

Developing Staff Skills

Employees are a restaurant's most important asset. They are also one of the biggest investments that restaurants incur. It is rare for people to be productive on their first day of work or if they are assigned new responsibilities. To increase productivity among all your staff and make them capable of implementing your marketing plans, you will need to provide ongoing training. Training comes in both informal and formal methods.

- **The informal approach**—In this approach, you assign a new employee to follow a veteran or seasoned employee around as this expert works. This approach enables the new employee to observe how the job is actually done. The advantage of this type of training for you is the small amount of time you spend with the trainee; the fact that someone else is spending time training means that you do not have to do it. The main disadvantage with the informal approach is that the new hire is learning from an individual who most likely has learned shortcuts and incorrect methods along the way; therefore, the new hire sometimes is learning the wrong things.

- **The formal approach**—In this approach, you establish a written training plan and training materials that describe what will be achieved, how it will be achieved, and when will it be achieved. This plan is implemented by you or another employee. Monitoring and follow-up should be conducted by you as the manager.

When and on What to Train

How do you know when training is needed? In general, it is probably needed every time an individual has new responsibilities or is newly hired. Actually, training should be continuous throughout each person's employment; after all, there is always something that can be done better, faster, or cheaper.

Another common question is, "On what does your staff need to be trained?" To answer this question, you must determine the **training gap**—the difference between current skills and desired skills. (See *Exhibit 3r.*) You determine employees' current job skills and knowledge through testing, observation, questioning, or surveying them. This is kind of like doing a SWOT analysis on employee capabilities. This process pinpoints the gaps in their job knowledge and skills.

Think About It...

Have you ever been in a class that covered things you already knew? How did that make you feel?

Exhibit 3r

Training Gap

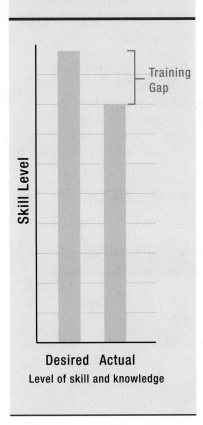

Training Gap

Skill Level

Desired   Actual
Level of skill and knowledge

The purpose of determining the training gap is economy of action. You could be wasting a lot of time and money training employees on things they already know, not to mention boring them. And you might miss the real topics on which they need training. In other words, a little investigation focuses your efforts and resources onto the exact topics needed.

Components of a Good Training Program

To be effective, a training program needs to answer these questions:

- What must be done?
- Why must it be done?
- How should it be done?
- To what standards should it be done?
- What is the difference between these things and the trainee's current abilities?

You should monitor your training for effectiveness, and you should conduct follow-up observation for all training participants. Upon completion, you should document the training results.

Setting Training Objectives

Once you have established the training gap, you should write specific objectives that address these deficiencies in skill and knowledge. Then you can target training to achieve these objectives. In order for objectives to be effective, they must be SMART:

- **S**pecific
- **M**easurable
- **A**chievable
- **R**elevant
- **T**imely

An example of a SMART objective involves recipe ingredients. More and more individuals are affected by food allergens, and one of the most common food allergens is peanuts. A SMART objective in regards to recipe ingredients could be that, by end of training, all employees will be able to name all menu items that contain peanuts or peanut oils.

Exhibit 3s

Training as an Investment

Training results in more skills and knowledge on the part of your employees.

These skills and knowledge result in more effectiveness and efficiency in employees' work performance and in improved customer interactions.

The improved work performance reduces cost and improves output, both of which lead to improved customer satisfaction and improved profitability.

The improved work performance and improved customer interactions directly improve customer satisfaction.

Improved customer satisfaction leads to increased revenues, increased profits, and greater employee satisfaction.

Increased profits enable you to take more money home and to make more investments in the operation.

Employee Training Is an Investment

Training is an employee investment with a good return. Although training costs money that might be scarce, good training ultimately returns to the operation more than its cost because it is utilized by trainees throughout their tenure. As a result, the restaurant benefits for years to follow. *Exhibit 3s* shows how it works.

As an example of investing in training your employees, say that you are the manager of the country club that serves Saddle River Salmon, and you want to increase sales of this item. There are several different investments you could make:

■ Conduct sales promotions (special price, advertising, two-for-one coupons, to name a few).

■ Use higher quality ingredients and advertise this fact.

■ Buy an improved grill for cooking the salmon (and other food).

■ Increase servers' knowledge of the Saddle River Salmon dinner through tasting, learning the ingredients, or other methods.

■ Increase servers' selling skills, so they can **upsell**—suggest a more expensive item—the Saddle River Salmon dinner.

Of course, you can do more than one or all of these at the same time. Suppose you decide to invest in sales skills training for your service employees. When successfully completed, the training investment will result in more sales skills for your service employees. These skills will be used immediately and for years to come in positively impacting sales. This will lead to happier customers, more customers, more and larger tips, and happier employees.

Although training is expensive, it is an investment that actually can provide a good return over several years. Time is the most expensive aspect of training because there are several people involved and there are considerable hours required to do a good job. Time is spent by the trainer on developing the training itself and on instructor preparation, program delivery, and training follow-up. Time is spent by employees on the lost work time of the trainees (or alternatively, on the other employees who must fill in for them while they are in training).

The time and effort you put into developing your employees are some of your most valuable investments, not expenses. An expense is an expenditure that is used in a short period of time such as a week, a month, or a year. Developing your employees is an investment because it returns benefits over a long period of time, usually many years.

In your marketing plan, you should include a budget line for training. Another budget line you should include is for promotion expenses.

Establishing Your Promotion Budget

The plan you develop for your promotions will need to be based on a budget. This budget may be determined during or after you develop your promotional plan. Promotion budgets are usually based on one of four methods:

- Estimate of what the business can afford after other costs are paid

- Percentage of actual or forecasted sales

- Amount spent on promotions by competitors of the business

- Promotion plan objectives and the actions needed to achieve them

The first two methods, what the business can afford and the percentage of sales, are the simplest methods you can use to determine a promotion budget. However, in both cases, if sales or revenue drop, your promotion budget shrinks. Such a budget reduction comes at the worst time since you need to promote your restaurant even more when sales and revenue are down.

Basing your promotion budget on the amount your competitors spend on their promotions is also relatively simple as long as you have access to this information. You can get an idea of this by researching industry averages. This method "levels the playing field" or provides a competitive foundation for your marketing communications. However, the information your competitors use to determine their promotion budgets may not apply to your restaurant.

The final method, basing your promotion budget on the promotion plan's objectives, helps to keep marketing efforts focused on those objectives. This method is the ideal one to use; however, it is also the most complex method. (Chapter 5 discusses promotion plans in more detail.)

When entering into a new operation or making plans for an existing operation, it is critical to plan out all the costs of the products and services to be provided. This must be balanced against the potential for revenue that the chosen target market can provide and that your operation can win from the competition. This leads, inevitably, to planning the operation's finances and feasibility.

Conducting a Feasibility Study

An analysis that is important to the overall success of your restaurant's marketing plan is a **feasibility study.** This kind of study is a compilation of data made before introducing a new product or opening a new operation to see how successful it will be.

Simply put, the study should answer the following questions:

- Will my business or new product work?

- Will my business or new product make money after expenses?

There are short-term and long-term feasibility plans. For a new operation, a typical long-term feasibility study includes the following sections:

1. Description of business concept, product, or service

   - ☐ Restaurant concept

   - ☐ Location

2. Assessment of market for business, product, or service

   - ☐ Market area

   - ☐ Population characteristics

   - ☐ Target market

   - ☐ Competition

3. Estimate of basic financial feasibility

   - ☐ Potential sales revenues

   - ☐ Fixed and variable costs

   - ☐ Budget

   - ☐ Anticipated operating profit

   - ☐ Investment break-even points

4. Problems and solutions

   - ☐ Identification of difficulties

   - ☐ How to overcome them

5. Assessment of capabilities to implement the business concept, product, or service

   - ☐ Prior experience

   - ☐ Skills and knowledge

   - ☐ Available assistance

6. Final analysis of feasibility

7. Final recommendation for or against the item studied

Setting Financial Goals

When you invest in something, you anticipate a **return on investment**—benefits received from an investment. Your investment can be in time, materials, or money. Your benefits can be in many forms, such as money, physical assets, services, market development, and good will. You can easily convert the value of time, materials, assets, and services into dollars. You will have difficulty converting the values of market development and good will into dollars, but their values are real, nonetheless.

In the restaurant business, you invest in facilities, equipment, tools, food supplies, promotion, and people in order to receive sales and profits in return. For a startup operation, the two largest investments are facilities and equipment. But over the long term, the two largest investments a restaurant has are food supplies and employees.

Selecting a Target Margin

An important financial goal to set for your restaurant is your target margin. Margin is another way to think of profitability. **Margin** is the percent of sales that is left after raw materials (food costs) and production costs (direct labor) have been subtracted; sometimes margin is called **gross profit.** In essence, margin is profit before controllable expenses, such as wages, utilities, and maintenance, and noncontrollable expenses, such as rent, insurance, and property taxes, have been subtracted. You can have a margin for the entire operation, you can have a margin for a category of food or beverage, and you can have a margin for individual menu items. Some of the business decisions that should be made are the desired margins for each of these, called your **target margins.**

Which Investment to Make

All forms of benefits should be considered when weighing an investment, not just the monetary benefits. For example, if you were to hire a catering manager to handle and sell events, your specific return on investment would be the improved effectiveness and efficiency of your catering operation, the customer satisfaction that results from this, and the increased sales from the additional events that were sold by the catering manager. Only the latter of these can be easily measured in monetary terms, but all three are valuable benefits.

As part of planning, you must decide what to invest in and how much to invest. These are interrelated, of course. To help you make these decisions, you should perform some investment calculations.

Investment Calculations

When your return on your investment can be translated into monetary terms, you can do calculations for both planning and evaluation purposes. There are several key types of calculations to make:

- Payback period

- Payback ratio

- Return on investment (ROI)

These calculations should be made before investing to help decide whether the investment is a good one to make and after the returns have been realized to see how well you did.

Payback Period

The **payback period** is the length of time taken for the investment to pay for itself.

Dollars invested ÷ **Dollar return per year** = **Payback period in years**

For example, if you invest $8,000 for a new grill and it improves your cook's efficiency so that you save $2,000 per year, your payback period is four years.

$8,000 ÷ $2,000 per year = 4 years

Payback Ratio

The payback ratio is better than the payback period because it shows how much the investment is worth—what it will yield. The **payback ratio** is the ratio of money returned over the life of the investment to the amount of the investment.

Lifetime dollars returned ÷ **Dollars invested** = **Payback ratio**

If the grill in the above example continues to return $2,000 per year for ten years, it would earn $20,000 over its lifetime. The payback ratio is 10:1.

$20,000 ÷ $2,000 = 10

Return on Investment

The favored calculation to use to evaluate an investment is the return on investment because it shows how much the investment yields in percentage form. Because of the percentage, the ROIs of several investments can be easily compared; all other things being equal, the one with the higher ROI is the better investment.

The **return on investment (ROI)** is the percent version of the payback ratio.

Lifetime dollars returned $\div$ **Dollars invested** $\times$ **100%** $=$ **ROI %**

The ROI in the previous example is 1,000%.

$20,000 $\div$ **$2,000** $\times$ **100%** $=$ **1,000%**

It looks like the investment in the improved grill is a very good one based on the figures that were used.

Setting the Financial Goals

Now that you can look at the possible investments objectively, you can decide what kinds of investments to make and what returns you hope for. The returns should be stated in dollars and cents, payback period, payback ratio, or ROI whenever possible. These returns are your financial goals.

Once you set financial goals along with all the other planning, you have a marketing plan. But there is one last thing to do before you start implementing the plan for your operation.

Activity

Your Financial Picture

You completed detailed plans for your new restaurant and determined that your startup costs would be $150,000. You predict that you will have revenue and expenses as follows:

Startup: $150,000

Year 1: revenue of $100,000, expenses of $85,000
Year 2: revenue of $200,000, expenses of $150,000
Year 3: revenue of $250,000, expenses of $187,500
Year 4: revenue of $300,000, expenses of $225,000
Year 5: revenue of $400,000, expenses of $247,500

1 **What is the payback period?** _____

2 **What is the ROI?** _____

Planning to Evaluate

As with any business, a restaurant's goal is to increase sales while decreasing expenses. The planning process is the tool to achieve this. However, planning means nothing if the plan is not implemented well and if the results have not been analyzed and evaluated. The evaluation stage of the planning process is a strong determiner of your successes and failures in achieving your measurable objectives. The best evaluations are those that are planned prior to being implemented; they should be part of your plan. (See *Exhibit 3t*.)

Exhibit 3t

Evaluations should be part of your marketing plan.

Many people have discovered that it is better to plan how you will collect and evaluate data before you begin implementing your plan. When you do this, several good things happen:

- **You discover errors and omissions in your plan.** When you think about the data you can collect, you often find that you did not include those factors or results in your plan. For example, if you are planning to evaluate a newspaper advertising campaign, you may discover that you forgot to include a way to track changes in sales after the campaign begins.

- **You put in place the tools to collect the data you need.** If you need to separate data differently than normal so you can evaluate an element of your plan, this is the time to discover that. For example, if you are planning a coupon promotion, you must make provisions to count the coupons used in each day part, annotate the coupons with the menu items served to indicate for which ones the coupons were used (if applicable), and save the coupons themselves with a date and time stamp. Otherwise, you will end up with a handful of coupons for which you know nothing but the overall number used.

■ **You firm up goals in the terms you are able to collect data for, especially making them quantitative.** For example, rather than hoping for "increased revenue due to the use of coupons" as a goal, you can say that revenues on day parts in which coupons are used will increase by 10 percent.

Once you have done marketing research, decided on a restaurant concept, selected target markets, decided on the products and services to offer, planned how to implement them, set financial goals, and planned how to evaluate everything, you finally are ready to implement your plan.

Summary

Developing a strategy for your business is the most effective and efficient way to address the market potentials and be successful. Developing a marketing strategy is critical. This involves selecting your target markets, determining your product positioning in the target markets, and preparing your value propositions for the target markets. Breaking the total market into segments allows you to concentrate on one or a few similar segments and use target marketing. To do this, you must narrow your focus to target markets you can serve and that will generate sufficient revenues for you to operate profitably. There are several strategies for addressing your target markets, and you must choose the one that is best for your situation.

Once you have identified your target markets and their needs, you can develop the products and services that will meet those needs and that can provide you a profit.

It is rare to be the first into a market, so most operations must position their products and services to compete with existing market leaders and other competitors. Product positioning is the term used for determining how to do this. A related aspect to this is the value proposition that spells out the benefits that your products and services can provide to your target market.

Obviously, to be able to position your products and services, you first must design them. In the restaurant and foodservice industry, there are many choices for type of operation, type of cuisine, and type of service. Also, you must decide on the exact products and services to provide.

Then you must plan your operating details such as processes, tasks, and standards. These include recipes, plating standards and many other things. These decisions will be put into operation shortly in decisions about facilities, equipment, staffing, and staff development.

You also need to determine when and how much to budget for promotions. You can base this budget on an estimate of what your restaurant can afford, a percentage of actual or forecasted sales, an estimate of what your competitors spend, or your promotion plan.

When all these decisions have been made, you are ready to document them and other things in your marketing plan: a description of your market area, target markets, market trends, competition, competitive advantage, marketing objectives, and financial objectives. Plan your work and work your plan. This is such a simple, though very important, phrase. Since restaurant work is often chaotic, it is important to have a plan that you can execute day in and day out to market your operation.

Once you have prepared the plan, you should plan how to evaluate it so you can identify what worked and what did not, and next time, what to repeat and what to do differently. That way, you will be able to understand why you did or did not achieve your goals.

Finally, you should prepare a feasibility study to determine whether your plan will actually have a chance in the market. It also is used to explain to investors how you can make money for them.

Effective planning and effective execution of the plan are key to a successful restaurant or foodservice operation.

Review Your Learning

1 All of the following are steps of a marketing strategy *except*

   A. determine target market.

   B. determine features and benefits.

   C. determine value proposition.

   D. determine product positioning.

2 All of the following are characteristics of useful market segmentation *except*

   A. maleable.

   B. identifiable.

   C. substantial.

   D. accessible.

3 Focusing your products and services on the needs of a single market segment is called

   A. market segmentation.

   B. product positioning.

   C. value proposition.

   D. target marketing.

4 Serving a specific market is an example of

   A. a target market strategy.

   B. effective product positioning.

   C. a value proposition.

   D. market segmentation.

5 Developing your value proposition is important because

   A. it is required by law.

   B. it completes your marketing research.

   C. it improves the quality of your products and services.

   D. it focuses your promotional efforts.

6 A marketing plan is a

   A. list of marketing activities that a restaurant can anticipate spending money on.

   B. document that will help you market your restaurant in order to increase business.

   C. document addressing the needs of the operation in order to operate efficiently.

   D. plan specifically identifying and setting your restaurant apart from the competition.

7 All of the following are elements of a marketing plan *except*

   A. competitive advantage.

   B. target market.

   C. feasibility study.

   D. market trends.

8 The purpose of a feasibility study is

   A. to show your preparedness to investors.

   B. to estimate whether your concept or product will work.

   C. to see whether your restaurant is well organized.

   D. to evaluate your preparedness for emergencies.

9 Your competitive advantage is

   A. what makes you different from your competition.

   B. competitive spirit.

   C. the advantages your competitors have over you.

   D. the type of competitors your restaurant has.

continued on next page

Review Your Learning *continued from previous page*

10 Determining the training gap is important because

A. productivity is inversely related to the amount of training.

B. managers enjoy training about topics they know a lot about.

C. employees are more easily trained when they can see the final result.

D. training only on the necessary topics is most efficient.

11 Which is *not* a true statement about positioning your product in the market?

A. Market positioning is getting your product noticed.

B. When positioning your product, you must highlight its unique and special qualities.

C. If your product is first to the market, you do not have to position it.

D. To effectively position your product when you are not the market leader, you must either attack the market leader or differentiate your product.

12 Which is *not* a true statement about planning to evaluate your marketing effectiveness?

A. Planning the evaluation ensures that your marketing plan will be implemented properly.

B. Planning the evaluation helps uncover errors and omissions in your plan.

C. Planning the evaluation ensures that you include the tools and procedures for tracking your plan's effectiveness.

D. Planning the evaluation helps firm up your marketing goals in quantitative terms.

Setting Prices

4

Inside This Chapter

- Choosing a Pricing Strategy
- Differentiators
- External Considerations When Pricing
- Internal Considerations When Pricing
- Calculating Prices

After completing this chapter, you should be able to:

- List and explain eleven pricing strategies.
- Explain how to gain a competitive advantage.
- Identify five external and six internal factors that affect your prices.
- Describe a competitive analysis.
- Calculate prices using the four pricing methods.
- Explain pricing psychology.

Test Your Knowledge

1 **True or False:** Your pricing strategy is determined by the location of your restaurant. *(See p. 81.)*

2 **True or False:** An external factor considered in pricing is competition. *(See p. 85.)*

3 **True or False:** A competitive analysis looks at other restaurant or foodservice establishments that offer similar products. *(See p. 86.)*

4 **True or False:** Bundling is how a product is packaged for shipping. *(See p. 90.)*

5 **True or False:** Setting menu item prices is simply a calculation of costs and desired profit. *(See p. 81.)*

Key Terms

À la carte menu

Actual cost pricing method

Competitive analysis

Competitive pricing method

Covers

Direct labor cost

Extensive menu

External factors

Factor pricing method

Fixed cost

Food cost

Food cost percentage

Limited menu

Prime cost pricing method

Profit

Profit margin

Pricing strategy

Rate of return

Standardized recipe

Target fixed cost percentage

Target food cost percentage

Target labor cost percentage

Target profit

Target variable cost percentage

Value perception

Variable costs

Think About It...

Why does one restaurant charge $2.50 for a hamburger and another one charge $8.50? How many reasons can you think of?

Introduction

Owning a restaurant is a dream many people have. This dream can be a reality if you offer products and services that your customers want at a price they are willing to pay and that still provides a reasonable profit. There are many factors to control and decisions to make in operating a successful restaurant or foodservice operation; one of them is the price you charge.

The restaurant industry is quite competitive. There are restaurants that offer great menu items and great services but never make enough money to stay in business. The difference between a dream and reality in the restaurant business is the ability to make enough money to stay open. Your ability to do this is directly affected by the quality of your pricing decisions. This chapter will help you make good pricing decisions.

Pricing is one of the four major elements of marketing (the four Ps). Pricing is an important strategic issue because it affects product positioning, menu, features, and promotion of your operation. In other words, it affects almost everything figured in dollars.

Choosing a Pricing Strategy

There are several methods and considerations that need to be addressed when pricing a product. Before beginning to price menu items, you should choose a **pricing strategy**—a rule that guides you in setting prices, also known as a pricing objective.

Your pricing strategy is determined by your marketing plan. For example, if pursuing a plan to increase your profitability, one of your strategies would be to increase your guest check average. In this case, you would want to consider raising prices wherever and whenever possible as well as utilizing upselling techniques. On the other hand, if you are planning to penetrate or dominate your target market, you would want to increase your **covers**—the number of guests in your restaurant—by attracting customers with lower prices or better service. Or, if trying to increase the number of repeat visits to your restaurant, you may want to offer coupons or institute another promotion program, which in turn would possibly affect the prices of some menu items. Whatever your marketing strategy, your pricing strategy should be consistent with it.

Developing a pricing strategy can also be determined by your business philosophy; *Exhibit 4a* shows two different business philosophies. For example, to make your restaurant very exclusive, setting prices higher than any of your competitors might be effective.

Another important consideration is what your customers expect from your menu items and what they are willing to pay for those items. For example, if you have a

Exhibit 4a

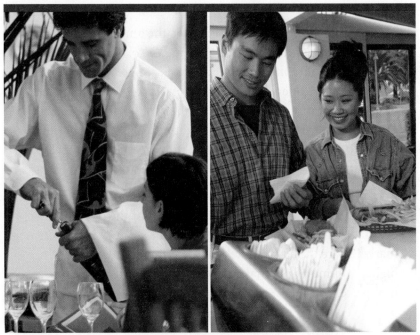

These two restaurants have different marketing goals and different pricing strategies.

Exhibit 4b

It is important to have a pricing strategy and that everyone on your team knows what it is.

steakhouse, do your customers anticipate prime or choice steaks? If they expect prime steaks, then you can and should charge a higher price. However, if your customers simply do not care about the difference between prime and choice steak, then your customers will not see the value in paying for prime.

Yet another consideration is how you want your business perceived by the public. You may want your restaurant to be considered a good value; in this case, your prices should be in the middle of the prices of your competitors. You are not striving to be the lowest-priced restaurant in the market; rather, you are aiming to be the value leader.

You must have a pricing strategy to guide your decisions. Additionally, everyone at your establishment responsible for setting prices should be using the same pricing strategy. (See *Exhibit 4b.*)

Common Pricing Strategies

There are many different strategies about what to accomplish with your pricing. Some pricing strategies are directed at what might be called ordinary situations. Others are special pricing strategies done temporarily for a special purpose. Following is a discussion of some of the most common ones.

Pricing Strategies for Ordinary Situations

Here are pricing strategies that you can use to guide pricing decisions for most economic and competitive situations:

- **Maximizing current profit—Profit** is the amount of money left after costs are subtracted from revenue. If costs are less than revenue, you have made money. If costs are greater than revenue, you have lost money. You can maximize profit by selling either a large number of meals at a low per-meal profit, or a smaller number of meals at a high per-meal profit. Be careful about trying to maximize current profits; it may result in lower long-term profits.

- **Maximizing current revenue—**By adopting this strategy, you try to maximize current revenue whether or not the operation is profitable. The primary reason to use this strategy is to increase market share. It may also help in lowering costs because at a higher volume of purchasing you can buy goods at a lower per-unit price.

- **Maximizing quantity**—With this strategy, your goal is to maximize the number of meals served or the number of customers served in order to increase the size of your operation. This will spread your fixed costs over more customers, thereby making the costs per customer smaller. It also will enable you to purchase supplies at a lower unit cost because of your increased volume of purchasing.

- **Maximizing profit margin**—This strategy is similar to maximizing profits. A **profit margin** is the percentage of revenue that goes to profits, typically on a per-unit basis. It is the amount remaining after paying the cost of food, and can be used for running the business. You would try to maximize the unit profit margin if you are in a low-volume operation.

- **Claiming quality leadership**—By adopting this strategy, you do everything you can to be seen as the quality leader. The most common way is to set a high price to indicate that your menu items are of high quality. In many people's eyes, a high price positions your products and operation as the quality leader.

- **Recovering total or partial cost**—This strategy means that you merely are trying to recover all or a certain fraction of your costs, not make a profit. You would use this pricing strategy if you were part of another organization that has other revenue sources; for example, a corporate employee-dining service.

- **Maintaining the status quo**—In this strategy, you try to achieve price stabilization in order to avoid price wars. This allows you to achieve a moderate but steady profit as long as you keep costs low enough.

- **Pricing for new customers**—This strategy is done routinely to attract new customers by offering some price incentive such as a discount or a two-for-one deal. This strategy is a permanent strategy but of limited application: for new customers only.

Temporary Pricing Strategies for Special Purposes

These strategies are used because of the current market, competition, or a profitability situation. As soon as appropriate, you will want to change to one of the ordinary strategies.

- **Survival**—If your market has declined, the market has too many competitors, or your profits are low, your goal may be to set prices that will cover costs and enable you to remain in the market. If this is your situation, survival would be more important than profit. This is a special pricing strategy that should only be a temporary one.

■ **Cream skimming**—This pricing strategy attempts to "skim the cream" off the top of the market by setting a high price and selling to those customers who are less price sensitive or early adopters—those who must have the newest thing. Skimming is most appropriate when you have a menu item that no competitor has, especially a newly invented one.

■ **Penetration pricing**—With this pricing strategy, your objective is to maximize the quantity of meals or customers served by offering a really low price, perhaps even selling at a loss. This strategy is used when competition is strong at present or expected to be in the near future. It is most appropriate when customers are price sensitive. It is best if the product being offered can bring in many customers fairly quickly so that the period of low prices is short. This is another special pricing strategy that should be used only temporarily.

As you can see, the different pricing strategies vary greatly from each other. But selecting a pricing strategy cannot be done in a vacuum. You must consider how your products differ from those of your competitors.

Activity

Actual Uses of Pricing Strategies

For each of the ordinary and special pricing strategies listed below, think of a business that seems to be using the strategy.

1 Maximize current profits _____

2 Maximize current revenue _____

3 Maximize quantity _____

4 Maximize profit margin _____

5 Claim quality leadership _____

6 Recover cost _____

7 Maintain status quo _____

8 New customer _____

9 Survival _____

10 Cream skimming _____

11 Market penetration _____

Exhibit 4c

A great location can entice customers to choose your establishment.

Differentiators

Differentiating your restaurant's products and services enables you to promote reasons why customers should choose to dine at your establishment versus your competitors' operations. Examples of possible differences include:

- Signature items that only you offer

- Different or specialized features

- Highly capable chef and staff

- Unique décor

- Great location (such as a scenic view of a lake; see *Exhibit 4c*)

- Extras (such as a cruise with the meal)

The differences in what is offered, both products and services, relate directly to the value of what customers purchase. The additional offerings of a fine-dining restaurant include higher quality food, higher quality recipes, décor, more involved service, etc. When more is offered, more can be charged as long as it is valued by the customers. In fact, more *must* be charged so that the greater costs of additional offerings can be covered by revenue.

All this must be taken into account when setting prices. But it is not as simple as merely covering obvious costs and ending with a little profit. There are other considerations.

External Considerations When Pricing

You should consider **external factors**—conditions outside your control—when pricing your menu items. External factors include such things as:

- Competition

- Economy

- Target market changes

- Community

- Food trends

- Seasonality of product

- Weather

- Laws and license requirements

- Taxes and fees

- Technological advancements

Your Competitors Affect Your Prices

The adage "Keep your friends close and your enemies closer" demonstrates the importance of knowing your competitors. If you do not know who your competitors are and do not learn what they offer, you will have a difficult time countering them. In your market research, you should have identified your competitors. Before you set prices, you should know what your competitors charge for their products and services.

An important step in understanding your competitors is to conduct a **competitive analysis.** This type of analysis looks at other establishments that offer similar products. The analysis lists what specific products these restaurants offer, the characteristics (e.g., weight, size) of the items, and their prices. When reviewing your competitors' prices, you may not want your prices to be too high, nor do you want them to be at the low end of the pricing scale, depending on your pricing strategy. An example of this type of analysis is shown in *Exhibit 4d*.

Exhibit 4d

Competitive Analysis of Entrées

Restaurant	Filet, 8 oz	Hamburger, 1/2 lb	Ribs, full slab	Veal, 7 oz	Salmon, 9 oz	Prime rib, king cut	Roast Chicken, half of whole	Tuna, 8 oz
Branson Chophouse	$ 18.50	$ 9.00	$ 13.50	$ 19.00	$ 20.50	$ 24.00	$ 10.50	$ 23.00
Will's Steakhouse	21.50	7.50	N/A	20.00	16.95	31.00	13.50	26.00
Carriage House	15.95	9.00	16.50	18.00	18.00	N/A	11.50	22.00
The Lantern Seafood and Steakhouse	21.00	9.00	18.50	22.00	17.50	N/A	16.50	28.00
The Coventry	26.50 (9 oz) 19.00 (6 oz)	8.00	19.50	21.00	19.50	29.00	11.50	25.00
Your Steakhouse	$ 23.50	$ 7.50	$ 21.50	$ 20.00	$ 18.50	$ 27.00	$ 11.95	$ 19.00

Suppose you are a manager whose competitive set includes the establishments listed in *Exhibit 4d,* and your pricing strategy is to price menu items competitively. After reviewing this information, you realize that your prices are in line for the filet, hamburgers, veal, salmon, prime rib, and chicken. However...

■ Your full slabs of ribs are priced too high. You may want to consider lowering your price to fall between $17.00 and $18.00.

■ Your tuna is priced considerably lower than that of your competitors. You could raise your price to fall between $24.00 and $25.00.

Keep in mind that *Exhibit 4d* looks only at entrées. You also must do a competitive analysis of the prices of supplementary products like appetizers, desserts, wine, beer, other special beverages, meal-sized salads, and all other substantial items.

It is not only your competitors' prices and services that affect your ability to set prices and make a reasonable profit. Other external factors that you must consider are the state of the economy, market trends, food trends, and the seasonality of your products.

Activity

Competitive Analysis

Select three restaurant or foodservice operations of the same type (quick service, family, fine dining, etc.). Obtain copies of their menus or visit the restaurants and copy the names, prices, and ingredients of their entrées. Prepare a competitive analysis of these restaurants' entrées like the one in this chapter.

The Economy Affects Prices

Some experts say that the restaurant industry is economy-proof because everyone has to eat. However, it is *where* people eat that is important to you as the manager of a restaurant. Following are some questions you should answer concerning the economy and how it affects your operation:

■ How is the quality of life in your market area?

■ Do people have jobs?

■ Are people spending their discretionary income—income that is available for people to spend after expenses are paid?

■ If so, how are they spending it?

If the economy is not doing well, people may be less inclined to eat out, especially if your prices are too high.

Unfortunately, terrorism plays a role in the economy. Following the events that occurred on September 11, 2001, the general economy was considerably down. Due to fears of the unknown, people were more cautious about where they spent their money. Many segments of the restaurant industry were negatively affected, such as high-priced restaurants. However, one segment did remarkably well during this period: local neighborhood restaurants that offered comfort food. These establishments grew in popularity due to the types of food they offered and the reasonable prices for those products. In general, people need to be with other people in times of despair, and these local restaurants provided this.

Exhibit 4e

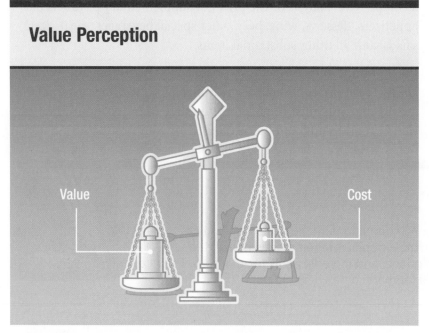

Value Perception

Value   Cost

Customers must weigh the value of your products against the cost of obtaining them.

Value Perception Affects Prices

Understanding your customers and their spending habits will assist you in establishing prices. A restaurant operator must know customers' **value perception**. Simply put, this is what a customer will willingly pay for a product or service. All customers want to feel they received a good value for their purchase; what that means is different for each customer. Each time a customer makes a buying decision, the customer must weigh the value of the product and its services against the cost of obtaining them. (See *Exhibit 4e*.) The cost includes more than money; it also includes time, effort, etc. The market research and market segmentation you did earlier will supply the information you need for these decisions.

One way customers feel that they are receiving value is through bundling—combining several menu offerings under one price, typically a price that is lower than the items purchased separately. The net result is a larger than average check and increased revenue because not all customers would have bought all of the items in the bundle. Quick-service restaurants do bundling effectively by offering "value meals" of a sandwich, side item, and soft drink for a set price. Other restaurants do this with fixed-price meals.

Service also can be bundled. The types and amounts of service bundled should be determined by what your market values are. For example, if you run a fine-dining restaurant in an affluent town, excellent service is not only important but necessary to get your customers to come back. If you feel that your customers value valet parking, you may want to provide this service on a complimentary basis. If you do this, you will need to incorporate the cost of the service into the menu prices.

You must determine whether or not particular services are valued by your target market. For example, if your customers are students, they may not care about complimentary valet parking. In fact, they may wish that you took that service away if doing so would lower menu prices.

Food Trends Affect Prices

Think About It...

What are some current food fads? Do you think any will become long-term trends?

Your prices also are affected by the popularity of what you sell. Popularity of food products tends to be one of four types: constant, a trend, a fad, or cyclic (e.g., seasonal).

Offering the right menu items at the right time at the right price can assist in realizing profits for an operation. Being on top of popular food trends might enable you to offer a trendy product at a premium price. For example, tiramisu recently was an extremely popular dessert, and due to the high demand for this product, restaurateurs were able to charge a premium price.

Food trends also can work against you if you invest in special equipment or training for a food trend that disappears. Two such food trends are Asian cooking and in-house microbreweries. Such food preparations require different equipment and skills. You should be wary of making a radical change in your operation unless you are sure that you can survive a possible decline in the trend.

Seasonality of Product Affects Prices

The seasonality of your food will determine what prices should be charged for them. There are various types of seasonality, such as agricultural seasonality, taste seasonality, and tourist seasonality. Depending on your pricing strategy, you can charge different prices when the food is in season or is in high demand. For example, you could charge higher prices when a product is in season because that is when it is usually the best quality or the only time it is available. Or, you might charge lower prices if your costs are lower when the product is in season. Conversely, when food items are out of season and you can still get them, you also might be able to charge a premium for providing them.

Internal Considerations When Pricing

Establishing a pricing strategy is directly associated with your goals for the restaurant, menu offerings, and staff skills. Setting and achieving goals are vital in determining your success or failure. All restaurant owners have the same high-level objectives: increase sales and decrease expenses. It is a matter of how and to what extent these goals are achieved that determines whether there is sufficient profit.

Financial Goals Affect Prices

You must establish what your profit should be as well as your costs. Remember: profit is the amount remaining after expenses are paid. **Target profit** is the amount of profit you hope to achieve. Another way to think of target profit is the return you want your investment to bring. **Rate of return** is the annual profit your investment earns or brings into your operation expressed as a perentage of your investment. Target profit and rate of return are important when you are trying to interest investors. They also are important when you are planning your operating budget and setting prices.

Recall that margin is the percentage of sales that is left after raw materials (food cost) and production costs have been subtracted. You must set prices so you realize your target margins. In fact, setting prices using target margins is easier than using net profits because you do not have to consider all the other costs that are part of controllable and noncontrollable expenses.

Predicted profits and margins usually will determine how customers are charged for their orders. You may decide to offer an **à la carte menu,** which means every item on the menu is priced individually. Or you may decide to bundle items to provide a better value for the customer and increase the average check.

Another way to increase profit is to reduce expenses. Then the amount you subtract from revenue is smaller and the bottom line result is larger. Most businesses try to do both.

Food Cost Affects Prices

Food cost is one of the major expenses of a restaurant or foodservice operation. **Food cost** is the cost of the food supplies used to make the menu items. The cost is for the form that you use (from bulk, uncut food to portion-controlled food that is ready to cook). This cost is for the food as delivered to your back door (transportation and taxes included).

Think About It...

What do you think is a fair profit percent for a restaurant? Is it different for different types of restaurants: quick service, family, fine dining, etc.?

In addition to the obvious costs, there are several other things included in food cost. (See *Exhibit 4f*.) These include:

- **Cost of food that is sold**—This is literally the cost of the food put on the plate.

- **Cost of preparation mistakes**—In every kitchen, there are mistakes that result in food being thrown away. While you try to minimize this, there always will be some mistakes.

- **Cost of food due to theft**—This is the cost of food stolen by employees, customers, or suppliers.

- **Cost of food wasted due to spoilage**—This is the cost of food that had to be discarded due to improper storage or excessive age.

Exhibit 4f

Food Cost Components

Food lost due to theft

Food lost due to spoilage

Food lost in preparation

Food used in menu item

The real cost of the food used in an operation contains several components.

All these food costs are added together to result in the overall food cost. It is very difficult to get accurate numbers for any but the first type of food cost, so food costs typically are done at a gross level. All these costs must be covered by revenue.

A single food cost is generally determined for an entire entrée or entire bundled order, rather than separate food costs for each of the parts. For example, perhaps a steak dinner consists of the steak plus potatoes, vegetable, side salad, and beverage. The food cost of the steak dinner is the sum of the food costs for all five of these items. Supplementary products like appetizers and desserts have individual food costs.

As previously stated, one goal in an operation is to reduce expenses. Since food cost is an expense, it should be reduced as much as is feasible while maintaining quality standards. Each type of food cost can be a target for expense reduction. The first food cost expenses to attack are those from theft and spoilage; these both are simply throwing money away. Then you can direct your attention to minimizing preparation waste and errors. One technique to reduce this kind of food cost is to use a **standardized recipe**—a recipe that gives a known quality and quantity at a known cost—and uses standardized portions.

The goal for many restaurants is to achieve a certain **food cost percentage,** which means that this percentage of the restaurant's revenue goes to the cost of purchasing food. Mathematically, food cost percentage is the food cost divided by the revenue generated. For example, the goal for many restaurants is to achieve a 33 percent food cost percentage; your operation's objective may be higher or lower depending on your pricing strategy.

Direct Labor Cost Affects Prices

The other main expense is labor, and it, too, should be scrutinized for ways to minimize its cost. **Direct labor cost** is the cost for preparing and serving each meal. The direct labor cost is figured by multiplying employees' hourly wage by the number of hours worked to prepare and serve a menu item. On average, restaurants strive to keep direct labor cost at or below a certain percentage, 30 percent for example.

The type of operation and the type of menu you have determine the number of staff you will need and their skill levels. For example, if an operation has an **extensive menu,** it has many menu items. Such an operation requires a more skilled staff because the many menu items are usually difficult to prepare. At the other extreme are operations with a **limited menu**—offering few items that usually are not difficult to prepare. This kind of operation requires fewer and less skilled staff.

General Operating Costs Affect Prices

Another area to consider is your restaurant's operating costs. These can be separated into controllable expenses and noncontrollable expenses. Controllable expenses include such items as management salaries and employee meals—basically, costs that managers can directly control. Noncontrollable expenses include rent and utilities—basically any cost over which managers have little or no control. (See the sample income statement in *Exhibit 4g.*)

Controllable and noncontrollable expenses should be determined first so you can see what financial resources are left for your food and labor costs.

Services Affect Prices

The services you provide affect the prices you can charge because the cost of providing them is an expense that revenue must cover. Services also are points of competition and should be subject to a

Exhibit 4g

Sample Income Statement

Statement of Income for Sally's Steaks
January 1, 2008 – January 31, 2008

	Amount	Sales %
Sales		
Food	$ 75,000	75.0%
Beverage	25,000	25.0%
Total sales	$100,000	100.0%
Cost of Goods Sold		
Food	$ 27,000	27.0%
Beverage	6,000	6.0%
Total cost of goods sold	$ 33,000	33.0%
Gross Profit		
Total gross profit	$ 67,000	67.0%
Direct Labor		
Total labor	$ 34,000	34.0%
Other Controllable Expenses		
Employee benefits	$ 2,600	2.6%
Management salaries	3,000	3.0%
Employee meals	400	0.4%
Accrued vacations and holidays	500	0.5%
Supplies	1,000	1.0%
Replacement china and flatware	400	0.4%
Linen rental	300	0.3%
Utilities	1,100	1.1%
Cleaning and sanitation	700	0.7%
Repairs and maintenance	900	0.9%
Advertising	800	0.8%
Music and entertainment	300	0.3%
Total other controllable expenses	$ 12,000	12.0%
Noncontrollable Expenses		
Rent	$ 6,100	6.1%
Insurance	2,200	2.2%
Property taxes	2,300	2.3%
Interest	600	0.6%
Depreciation	2,800	2.8%
Total noncontrollable expenses	$ 14,000	14.0%
Total expenses	$60,000	60.0%
Income before taxes	$ 7,000	7.0%
Taxes	$ 2,000	
Net income	$ 5,000	

competitive analysis. Services can be either charged or "free" (really, included in overall prices since you have to cover their costs). If services are charged for, you must decide whether to charge the full cost plus some profit, just the full cost, or less than the full cost with the remainder being considered a marketing expense.

In the example of the steak restaurant, your analysis of the services provided by your steakhouse competitors (see *Exhibit 4h* on the next page) is educational, as was the earlier competitive analysis of entrées. You are competitive in the provision of parking, coat check, doggie bags, family-style dining, and having a wine steward. However…

■ You are the only operation not providing valet parking. Because you have a small parking lot, your customers probably are having difficulty finding parking; if this is keeping them away from your operation, you are losing money. Since you cannot build a larger parking lot in your congested location, you really should provide a valet parking service. Whether it is free or for a fee depends on your other costs.

■ You are the only operation not using cloth linens. You should seriously consider using them to remain competitive.

■ You have a private room, which is better than Will's Steakhouse, but you charge a lot more for it than your other competitors. You should lower or eliminate your fee to remain competitive.

Exhibit 4h

Competitive Analysis of Services

Restaurant	Valet parking	Parking lot	Coat check	Doggie bags	Cloth linens	Family-style dining	Private room	Wine steward
Branson Chophouse	Free	No	$ 2.00	Yes	Yes	No	$ 50.00	No
Will's Steakhouse	$ 5.00	No	No	Yes	Yes	Yes	No	No
Carriage House	$ 8.00	Small	Free	Yes	Yes	No	Free	Yes
The Lantern Seafood and Steakhouse	$ 6.00	Large	No	Yes	Yes	Yes	$ 75.00	No
The Coventry	Free	Large	Free	Yes	Yes	No	Free	Yes
Your Steakhouse	No	Small	Free	Yes	No	Yes	$ 150.00	No

Styles of Service Affect Prices

Although the service style could be considered merely as one of your services, it is a major service decision and bears a little elaboration. Remember that when you planned your operation, you selected a style of service. (The four styles commonly used in the United States are Russian, French, English, or American.) Your pricing should cover the costs of the type of service you chose. For example, you would charge higher prices to account for the extra cost in providing either the Russian or French service styles. Conversely, you could charge lower prices if you implemented the American or, especially, the English service styles.

As mentioned previously, understanding the services, products, and prices of your competitors is important when determining your own prices. (See the competitive analysis of service style in *Exhibit 4i*.)

From your competitive analysis of service style in the steak restaurant example, you find that you are the only restaurant using the French style of service, which is the most elegant and expensive. Although expensive, the French style of service does set you apart from your competitors, and customers will expect to pay a higher

Exhibit 4i

Competitive Analysis of Service Style

Restaurant	Russian	French	English	American
Branson Chophouse			X	
Will's Steakhouse				X
Carriage House			X	
The Lantern Seafood and Steakhouse				X
The Coventry			X	
Your Steakhouse		X		

price for this type of service. The problem is that by using the French style of service you are receiving lower profits because you are not charging for the higher expenses. Considering this, you may want to consider either raising prices to account for the extra expenses or change to the Russian or American style.

Once you have selected a pricing strategy, decided on products and service, and done a competitive analysis of your products and services, you are ready to calculate the actual prices to charge. The next section explains several ways to do this.

Activity

Pricing Considerations and Strategies

Select three restaurants: one quick-service, one family, and one fine-dining restaurant. Do not select a chain quick-service restaurant because prices for these are set at corporate headquarters, not at the individual restaurants. Interview the owners or managers (whoever sets the menu prices) about their pricing considerations. Ask them to explain what external and what internal considerations they take into account when setting their prices; be prepared to ask about all of the considerations discussed in this chapter. List for them the pricing strategies from this chapter, and ask what strategy is the closest to what they are using, or find another way to get at this information. Also, try to find out who they see as their competitors.

Summarize your results and then draw conclusions about the similarities and differences in pricing considerations and strategies among the different types of restaurants. Do these restaurants see each other as competitors? What does the identity of their competitors seem to have to do with their pricing strategies?

Calculating Prices

There are many ways to actually calculate what price a restaurant can charge for a menu item. The most popular ones are the factor method, the actual cost method, the prime cost method, and the competitive method. But doing the calculations is not the most important part. You must understand the impact of the prices you charge.

- Prices determine how much revenue you can bring in, and this revenue must cover your expenses and leave a little for profit. Prices that are too low will result in too little profit.

- Prices influence which customers you attract and whether they even become customers.

- Prices affect customers' feelings of value—whether they received good value for what was spent. Prices that are too high or too low can direct customers to your competitors.

- Prices affect which menu items are selected and how many of each are sold. Since food and labor costs associated with individual menu items are seldom completely accurate, skewing the mix of menu items sold can affect overall profitability.

- Prices are subject to psychological interpretation. This is such an important point that it is addressed in the next section.

Pricing Psychology

People perceive prices mostly in terms of the first digit of the price. As a result, they perceive a price of $8.00 and a price of $8.99 as being about the same, even though they differ by almost one dollar. On the other hand, they perceive a price of $7.99 as very different from a price of $8.00, even though they differ by only a penny.

Conclusions you can draw from this are:

- Charge a price slightly under a "magic number": a whole dollar amount, a whole multiple of $10, etc. Do not charge a price greatly under a magic number (like $8.12) or you will be giving away revenue (the difference between $8.12 and $8.99).

- Even though you may calculate a price of $8.43, change this to a psychological price of $8.95 or $8.99 because prices in the restaurant industry customarily end in "95" or "99."

- If you have to raise prices, avoid raising prices to just over the next dollar. Instead, raise them by a whole dollar.

If you are not the quality leader, delay raising prices (even though you are not making much profit), until your competitors raise theirs. Then raise your prices by more than is needed for profitability to just under the next magic number. This will enable you to recoup your lost profits from the delayed price increase.

Always apply pricing psychology after you have calculated prices using one of the price calculation methods.

Think About It...

Is it just a coincidence that most prices end in "95" or "99'"?

Key Pricing Terms

Several terms are used throughout the pricing methods that follow. Here are their definitions:

- Food cost—Actual or estimated cost of the food in a menu item

- **Target food cost percentage**—Percentage of revenue that is ideal for food cost

- Labor cost—Actual cost of labor to prepare the menu item (usually only hourly labor, but sometimes management as well)

- **Target labor cost percentage**—Percentage of revenue that is ideal for labor cost

- Target margins—Profit margin that is your business (and pricing) goal

- **Variable costs**—Costs other than food and labor that change from month to month

- **Target variable cost percentage**—Percentage of revenue that is ideal for variable costs

- **Fixed costs**—Those operating costs that are relatively constant, such as rent, management salaries, etc.

- **Target fixed cost percentage**—Percentage of revenue that is ideal for fixed costs

Factor Pricing Method

In the **factor pricing method,** you set your prices to achieve a target food cost percentage on each item. Typical food cost percentages range from a low of 25 percent to a high of 50 percent. For the same actual food cost, a lower food cost percentage results in a higher menu price, and a higher food cost percentage results in a lower menu price. (See *Exhibit 4j* on the next page.) The calculation will demonstrate this.

Overall, in this method, you use your target food cost to derive a factor that you multiply each food cost by to arrive at a price. So, there are two steps in the factor method:

1 Determine the factor.

2 Apply the factor to calculate the price.

To determine the factor, use this formula:

100% ÷ Target food cost percentage = Factor

Exhibit 4j

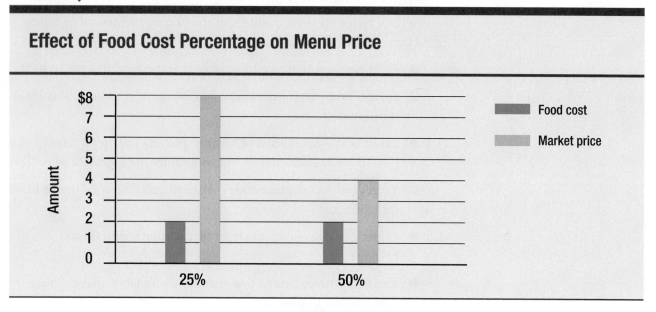

Effect of Food Cost Percentage on Menu Price

If your target food cost percentage is 33.3%, your factor is 3.00.

100% ÷ 33.3% = 3.00

To calculate prices, use this formula:

Food cost × Factor = Price

If your item's food cost is $3.26 and your factor is 3.00, your calculated price is $9.78.

$3.26 × 3.00 = $9.78

Remember: do not use only the calculated price; use pricing psychology to set the price at $9.95 or $9.99.

Actual Cost Pricing Method

The **actual cost pricing method** attempts to include the target profit for each cost element. In this method, the following cost elements are added together to total the calculated price:

■ **Food cost**—Actual or estimated cost of the food

■ **Total labor cost (hourly plus management)**—Cost of labor to prepare the menu item plus one preparation's share of management labor cost. For example, in the sample income statement in *Exhibit 4g* on p. 93, management salaries are $3,000. If 10,000 meals are sold in a year, $0.30 must be covered by each meal in addition to the actual cost of direct labor for that meal.

■ **Variable cost percentage**—Percentage of revenue that is used for variable costs. For example, in the sample income statement in

Exhibit 4g, controllable expenses are $12,000. Subtracting the $3,000 for management salaries, variable costs are $9,000. This is 9 percent of the $100,000 total sales amount.

■ **Fixed cost percentage**—Percentage of revenue that is used for fixed costs. For example, in the sample income statement in *Exhibit 4g,* the noncontrollable expenses are 14 percent of revenue.

■ **Profit percentage**—Percentage of revenue that was left as profit. For example, in the sample income statement in *Exhibit 4g,* income before taxes is 7 percent of total sales.

The easiest way to work with these numbers is to combine all the percentages into a single percentage. For the current example, 9 percent variable cost, 14 percent fixed cost, and 7 percent profit add up to 30 percent. Then you can use the following formula to obtain the calculated price:

$$\left(\text{Food cost} + \text{Total labor cost} \right) \times \left(100\% + \text{Combined percentage} \right) = \text{Price}$$

If the direct labor cost is $3.04 and the management labor cost is $0.30, the total labor cost is $3.34. If the food cost is $3.26, the calculated price is:

$$\left(\$3.26 + \$3.34 \right) \times \left(100\% + 30\% \right) = \text{Price}$$

$$\$6.60 \times 130\% = \text{Price}$$

$$\$8.58 = \text{Price}$$

Applying pricing psychology to the calculated price would result in a price of $8.95 or $8.99.

Prime Cost Pricing Method

The **prime cost pricing method** of calculating prices recognizes the fact that some menu items require large amounts of direct labor to prepare the food for cooking. This occurs when unprocessed ingredients are used, such as:

■ Side of beef that must be cut into steaks and roasts

■ Vegetables that must be washed, peeled, and chopped, before being used for salads or side dishes

■ Fried items that first must be breaded

■ Pastries that must be made from scratch ingredients

If these items were purchased already processed, these preparation costs would already be included in their costs.

In comparison, other items require little labor prior to cooking and plating, such as spaghetti, prime rib, and baked whole chicken. If you include the higher preparation costs to price these items, then they would carry the costs of the extra preparation.

The prime cost method adds the extra preparation costs only to those items that require it and uses an adjusted food cost percentage to calculate the price.

The formula for items with extra preparation is:

$$\left(\begin{array}{c} \textbf{Preparation} \\ \textbf{cost} \end{array} + \begin{array}{c} \textbf{Food} \\ \textbf{cost} \end{array} \right) \div \left(\begin{array}{c} \textbf{Preparation} \\ \textbf{labor} \\ \textbf{percentage} \end{array} + \begin{array}{c} \textbf{Target food} \\ \textbf{cost} \\ \textbf{percentage} \end{array} \right) = \textbf{Price}$$

For example, calculate the price of skirt steak where a side of beef is the starting point. The costs might be:

■ Food cost of the steak portion of the side of beef is $3.26.

■ Extra processing costs are $0.75 per steak.

■ Extra preparation labor is 7 percent of revenue.

■ Target food percentage is 33 percent of revenue.

Then the calculated price is:

$$(\ \textbf{\$0.75} + \textbf{\$3.26} \ ) \div (\ \textbf{7\%} + \textbf{33\%} \ ) = \textbf{Price}$$
$$\textbf{\$4.01} \div \textbf{40\%} = \textbf{Price}$$
$$\textbf{\$10.03} = \textbf{Price}$$

Using pricing psychology, you would set the price at $9.95 or $10.95.

Menu items without extra preparation use a simpler formula to get the calculated price:

Food cost ÷ Target food cost percentage = Price

In the same restaurant, you can also calculate the price of spaghetti, which has no extra processing labor. The costs might be:

■ Food cost of the spaghetti ingredients is $1.22.

■ Target food percentage is 33 percentage of revenue.

Then the calculated price is:

$$\textbf{\$1.22} \div \textbf{33\%} = \textbf{Price}$$
$$\textbf{\$1.22} \div \textbf{33\%} = \textbf{Price}$$
$$\textbf{\$3.70} = \textbf{Price}$$

Again, do not use the calculated price. Use pricing psychology to set the price at $3.95 or $3.99.

Competitive Pricing Method

The **competitive pricing method** is the easiest of all. There are no calculations. You simply use the prices of your best competitor. If you would rather, you can average the prices of several competitors.

Take note, however, that the competitive pricing method does not take into account *your* costs for food ingredients and labor. If your costs are significantly higher than your competitors' costs, you could actually lose money with this method.

Activity

Pricing Menu Items

You are in charge of setting the prices for menu items at Martha's Family Dining. Martha likes to have everything in her restaurant made from scratch. She even has an in-house butcher and an in-house baker. Martha has just added Old Fashioned Chicken Pot Pie to the menu. Your task is to determine the price.

You have learned about four methods of calculating prices and want to see which works best for the restaurant. The assignment to price the Old Fashioned Chicken Pot Pie is a wonderful opportunity to do just that.

You have asked for and Martha has given you the following information:

- Food cost: $3.47
- Target food cost percentage: 35%
- Direct labor cost: $2.85
- Management labor cost: $0.25
- Target direct labor percent: 32%
- Target management labor percent: 5%
- Target variable cost percent: 10%
- Target fixed cost percent: 12%
- Target profit percent: 9%
- Extra preparation cost: $0.95
- Extra preparation labor: 10%
- Prices at competing restaurants: $8.95, $9.99, $10.50, and $9.95

Determine the calculated menu price for the Old Fashioned Chicken Pot Pie by each of the following methods, and then set a price using pricing psychology for each calculated price.

	Calculated price	Menu price
1 Factoring method	_____	_____
2 Actual cost method	_____	_____
3 Prime cost method	_____	_____
4 Competitive method	_____	_____

Summary

Offering the best products and services does not guarantee success in the restaurant and foodservice industry. For financial success, you must develop business, marketing, and pricing strategies that take into account your competitors, your customers' dining preferences, and their willingness to spend money at your restaurant versus your competitors' restaurants.

You also must understand your own operation and the costs associated with it when establishing prices. Since food and labor costs usually represent more than 60 percent of a restaurant's operating budget, reducing one or both of these expenses will increase a restaurant's profitability. There are specific ways to decrease these expenses. Offering an American or English style of service can reduce labor costs. Providing a limited menu can also reduce costs because of fewer items and the simplicity of the menu items. Another way to decrease costs is to use standardized recipes and portions. This type of menu saves money because purchasing and preparation are controlled, which saves money in both areas.

Selling food and drink in such a way as to be profitable is the overall goal of a restaurant or foodservice operation. Implementing a pricing strategy is vital for achieving this goal. However, profit is not the only consideration. Several pricing strategies were described that pursued other objectives, such as market penetration and remaining competitive.

Four methods of calculating prices were described: the factor method, the actual cost method, the prime cost method, and the competitive method. In addition, prices should always be modified from a calculated amount to an amount that follows pricing psychology.

Review Your Learning

1 In a competitive analysis, you

  A. gather product and price information from competitors.

  B. gather quantities sold of similar products from your competitors.

  C. compare your expenses to those of your competitors.

  D. determine the overlap between your market area and that of your competitors.

2 All of the following are external factors to consider when establishing prices *except*

  A. type of menu.

  B. target market.

  C. economy.

  D. competition.

3 All of the following are external factors affecting prices *except*

  A. competition.

  B. food cost.

  C. taxes.

  D. food trends.

4 In the pricing strategy where your goal is to maximize quantity, you do all of the following *except*

  A. increase number of meals served.

  B. decrease unit costs.

  C. increase item profitability.

  D. decrease fixed costs per customer.

5 One way to gain a competitive advantage is

  A. offering a unique menu item.

  B. matching your competitors' offerings.

  C. meeting the prices of your competitors.

  D. implementing promotions regularly.

6 Food cost is

  A. the cost of the food for a menu item.

  B. all the costs of being in the food business.

  C. the overall cost of food purchased for the restaurant.

  D. the cost of putting an item on your menu.

7 In the pricing strategy where your goal is to penetrate a market, you do all of the following *except*

  A. increase the number of meals sold.

  B. decrease your prices.

  C. use this strategy for a short time.

  D. decrease your advertising costs.

8 All of the following are internal factors affecting prices *except*

  A. food trends.

  B. financial goals.

  C. food cost.

  D. style of service.

continued on next page

Review Your Learning *continued from previous page*

9 The principle of pricing psychology states that

A. people tend to ignore prices that are under $4.00.

B. people do not distinguish between prices within the same dollar amount.

C. people mostly choose the item with the lowest price.

D. people compare value received for price paid when they make all but the least significant purchases.

10 Your restaurant uses the factor method of pricing. Your target food cost is 30%. Your target variable cost is 20%. Your target fixed cost is 10%. Your target profit is 10%. Your target labor cost is 33%. The extraordinary processing of the item costs $0.60 and is normally 5%. If a menu item's food cost is $5.00, what is the calculated price?

A. $12.50   C. $16.65

B. $15.00   D. $25.00

Planning and Implementing Your Promotion Mix

5

After completing this chapter, you should be able to:

- List the benefits of promotions.
- Describe the components of the promotion mix.
- Describe how to create a promotion plan.
- List at least three benefits of public relations.
- Recognize different types of sales promotions.
- Describe methods of personal selling.
- Identify potential problems in implementing promotions.
- Identify reasons why employee training is part of a promotion plan.

Test Your Knowledge

1. **True or False:** You always pay for publicity. *(See p. 109.)*

2. **True or False:** Advertising can be seen as impersonal. *(See p. 117.)*

3. **True or False:** Promotions involve only contests and premiums. *(See p. 108.)*

4. **True or False:** Only designated sales staff should actually be selling. *(See p. 135.)*

5. **True or False:** The promotion mix includes advertising, sales promotions, personal selling, and public relations. *(See p. 108.)*

Key Terms

Advertising

Advertising campaign

AIDA

Bartering

Brainstorming

Clearinghouses

Commissions

Community relations

Contest

Cooperative advertising

Cooperative marketing

Cooperative sales
    promotions

Coupons

Deals

Exposure

Frequent diner programs

Mass media

Media

Media kit

Media relations

Media vehicle

Networking

News release

Personal selling

Point of purchase

Premiums

Press clipping bureaus

Press kit

Press release

Promotion mix

Promotion materials

Promotions

Public relations

Publicity

Publics

Reach

Reward programs

Sales promotions

Sales quota

Samples

Specials

Sponsor

Suggestive selling

Sweepstakes

Target audience

Trade-outs

Introduction

To attract customers, your restaurant can offer great customer service, wonderful ambience, an outstanding signature dish, and a popular theme. However, these important efforts are usually not enough to ensure that you have sufficient business. You must promote your restaurant; you must tell people about your customer service, ambience, dishes, and theme, and persuade them to patronize your establishment. But how do you get your message to the right people? This is the question the promotion mix addresses.

Today, everyone is bombarded with advertisements from all types of **media,** or forms of communication. These may be print media, such as newspapers, magazines, or direct mail; electronic media, such as television, radio, or the Internet; or other media, such as outdoor advertising. As a restaurant manager, you should understand how these media and other methods may be used to promote your business. To this end, understanding the **promotion mix**—a business's entire marketing communications program—is essential. The promotion mix is a vital element when planning a new restaurant, and it is useful for established restaurants as well.

Developing the best promotion mix for your restaurant will increase your overall success by providing many benefits:

- Attracting customers from your target market

- Increasing business in general and also during slow periods

- Introducing new menu items and showcasing existing menu items

- Making your restaurant more competitive

- Encouraging customers to purchase more

- Reinforcing or redefining your restaurant's image

The most effective way to get the best return on your investment in promotions and to make sure your promotions are successful is to create a promotion plan that defines your promotion mix and explains how to implement it. The promotion mix should complement your restaurant's marketing plan and objectives. You want to ensure that the image you convey for your operation and the components of the promotion mix adequately support each other. You want to choose advertisements and promotions that reflect the style and service of your establishment. For instance, if your restaurant is a full-service restaurant, then high-quality, professionally produced advertisements will convey an image more consistent with your operation than flyers from the local copy shop.

Developing an effective promotion mix requires good planning and implementation. Before you can learn how to do this, however, you must understand the components of the promotion mix.

Exhibit 5a

The Promotion Mix

Sales promotions

Advertising

Personal selling

Public relations

Components of the Promotion Mix

The communication that a restaurant establishes with the public is a critical link in its short-term and long-term success. There are various ways to communicate information about your restaurant to the public. To cover the multiple areas of communication, a manager needs to pay particular attention to the operation's promotion mix, which is comprised of advertising, sales promotions, public relations, and personal selling. (See *Exhibit 5a.*) Together or separately, these parts are also called **promotions.**

Advertising

Whenever marketing is discussed, advertising is also likely to be mentioned. However, while advertising may be part of a marketing plan, the two are not the same. In Chapter 1, you learned that marketing is the planning and execution of the concept, price, promotion, and distribution of products or services that influence sales and customer buying decisions while satisfying the objectives of the restaurant. Whereas, according the American Marketing Association, **advertising** is:

The placement of announcements and persuasive messages in time or space purchased in any of the mass media by business firms, nonprofit organizations, government agencies, and individuals who seek to inform and/or persuade members of a particular target market or audience about their products, services, organizations, or ideas.

The distinguishing features of advertising are:

■ It is a paid form of communication.

■ It uses **mass media**—communication that reaches a large audience—to deliver its message.

■ It has a **sponsor**—the business firm, nonprofit organization, government agency, or individual who purchases the advertising.

Good advertising is persuasive; it influences consumers' buying decisions by making people more aware of a business, product, or message.

Public Relations

Restaurants and other businesses have several **publics,** or groups of people in their market area and community. Customers are one of these groups. Other groups that can impact your business include your employees, people who work in media, public officials, and community organizations. The perception that these groups have of your business affects your ability to attract and keep customers, and this perception may even affect others who have a role in your business, such as suppliers, financiers, and investors.

While all the components of the promotion mix can affect public perception of your restaurant, one part of the mix, public relations, can be especially persuasive. **Public relations** is a form of marketing communications by which your business is promoted through **publicity**—communication that you do not pay for. Typically, publicity created through public relations appears in the form of newspaper, television, radio stories, or "plugs" by third-party sources, such as restaurant critics. Publicity also includes word-of-mouth communication.

Sales Promotions

Your advertising and other types of marketing communication will be most effective if you can offer your customers special incentives, or **sales promotions,** for patronizing your restaurant. Sales promotions come in many forms, such as coupons, contests, and giveaways. For example, if your target market is families, you might offer "free meals for children" coupons to parents and helium balloons to children.

Like advertising, sales promotions increase customer awareness of your restaurant or certain menu items. However, sales promotions usually provide customers with a more urgent incentive to patronize your restaurant, purchase a certain item, or otherwise change their spending behavior. Sales promotions typically offer the customer a benefit in exchange for his or her business, often within a limited time frame.

Note that in discussions on marketing, the term "promotions" is sometimes used interchangeably with the term "sales promotions." The use of "promotions" can cause confusion because the entire promotion mix also can be referred to as "promotions." To avoid any confusion, this guide uses "promotions" to mean any combination of components in the promotion mix and "sales promotions" specifically to mean sales promotions.

Exhibit 5b

Personal selling involves a meeting or interaction between a sales person and a prospective customer.

Personal Selling

The final portion of the promotion mix, **personal selling,** involves a meeting or interaction of two or more people for the purpose of exchanging information and making and closing a sale. (See *Exhibit 5b.*) Sometimes just called selling or sales, personal selling creates a relationship between the customer and the restaurant staff. This enables the staff to tailor the marketing message to the customer's individual needs. For example, a form of personal selling that is important for restaurants is upselling—when the server suggests higher-priced items to the buyer.

Exhibit 5c

Promotion Mix Planning

Identify audience.

Determine strategies and objectives.

Choose tactics.

Plan the implementation.

Planning the Promotion Mix

Determining the components of a promotion mix is only part of the process of developing effective marketing communications. To ensure your promotion plan supports the goals of your marketing plan, you must consider many aspects that can affect your promotions, and you must create a plan for your promotions. Your promotion plan should be based on the research you conducted during your situation assessment and feasibility study. You already should have researched both internal and external factors in your market environment, especially your target market and your competitors, before you even begin planning your promotion mix.

Assuming you have already done this research, the process of planning your promotion mix starts with identifying your **target audience**—the people you want your communications to reach. (See *Exhibit 5c.*) After this, you can begin to develop your communication strategies and objectives. This part of the process involves many aspects, such as assessing what customers already know about your restaurant or menu items, determining when to implement the communication, setting promotion objectives and measurements, and determining at a high level the message and image you want to communicate. All of these actions should support your restaurant's marketing plan. Once you have determined your promotion strategies and objectives, you can establish the proportion of the components in your promotion mix. Then you can choose the tactics that will best support your strategy:

■ For advertising and public relations, you choose the types of media for your communication.

■ For sales promotions, you choose the types of sales promotions.

■ For sales promotions and personal selling, you choose whom to sell to.

Once you have identified your tactics, you can begin planning the details for implementing your promotion.

As with marketing plans, you should document your promotion plan. Having a written plan helps you to focus your marketing communications efforts, so you do not waste time and money pursuing irrelevant or even counterproductive activities. A written plan also provides an essential foundation for tracking the results of your marketing efforts.

Identifying Your Audience

Before you begin planning your promotion mix, you should have already identified your target market and determined your marketing plan. As you begin planning your promotion mix, you also need to consider the target audience for your communication. Your restaurant's target market and target audience might be the same, or they might be different. For example, suppose your restaurant has three target markets: business people during lunch, seniors during dinner, and families during dinner. If the goal of your promotion mix is to increase sales during the lunch hour, your target audience is business people. However, if your target market is, for example, upper-middle-income tourists, one of your target audiences might be people who could recommend restaurants to your target market, such as hotel concierges, cab drivers, and tour guides.

Your target audience will drive every decision you make in your promotion plan. Therefore, you need to clearly profile your target audience, especially if it is different from your target market. Developing this profile may take additional research. Finally, depending on your marketing plan, target markets, and target audiences, you may need to develop multiple promotion plans.

Determining Your Promotion Strategies

Once you have identified the target audiences for your promotions, you can begin thinking about how to reach those audiences and what you want to convey with your promotions. To determine the strategies and objectives for doing this, you should consider several questions:

- How will the promotion plan support the overall marketing plan and objectives?

- Where is your restaurant or product in its product life cycle?

- When should the promotion start and end?

- What should the promotion accomplish (in measurable terms)?

- What message should the promotion communicate?

Exhibit 5d

A good promotional strategy requires many ideas.

To consider these questions, you must generate many ideas. Especially in the early planning stage, the more ideas you can come up with, the better the solutions you have to choose from. To get input from others, such as your staff, you can try **brainstorming**— a method for generating ideas in a group in which people volunteer ideas that are not evaluated until later. (See *Exhibit 5d.*) Throughout the planning process, you most likely will need to step back, revisit some of your decisions, and come up with more ideas. However, in all cases, your promotion strategy and objectives must support your marketing plan.

Supporting the Marketing Plan

Your promotion plan should align with and support your overall marketing plan. For example, if one of your marketing plan objectives is to increase sales of appetizers by 10 percent in the next six months, your promotion plan might focus on increasing awareness of certain appetizers through advertising, offering coupons or specials for appetizers, training servers to suggest appetizers, or generating publicity about your appetizer offerings. The promotion plan needs to support your marketing plan in all areas and account for all the information you researched about your market, including:

- Restaurant concept
- Market area
- Market summary
- Target markets
- Market trends

- Market growth
- Competitors
- Your competitive advantage
- Marketing objectives
- Financial objectives

Your marketing plan is based in part on where your restaurant or product is in its product life cycle. Similarly, the product life cycle also affects your promotion strategy.

Considering Your Product Life Cycle

A strategy for promoting a product must consider where the product is in its life cycle—introduction, growth, maturity, or decline. The product life cycle stages affect your promotional strategy in the following ways:

- **Introduction**—Building awareness of the product

- **Growth**—Building brand recognition and differentiating the product

- **Maturity**—Reinforcing customer preferences and customer loyalty

- **Decline**—Minimum promotions to remind customers of the product

Timing the Promotion

Another aspect that you must consider when creating a promotion plan is the timing of the components in your promotion mix. When should each type of promotion start and end? To answer this question, refer to your earlier research and your marketing plan objectives. Consider your target audience and the best ways and times to reach them. Also consider the day parts, holidays, or seasons identified by your marketing plan objectives.

Think About It...

To monitor publicity, some companies use **press clipping bureaus,** which are organizations that monitor the media and record any mention of a company or its products.

Setting Promotion Objectives and Measurements

Once you have considered various aspects of your promotion strategy, you are ready to begin developing objectives for your promotion. These objectives are a critical part of your promotion plan, and just like the ones developed for your marketing plan, the objectives must be reasonable, measurable, and have a time frame.

The objectives also must align with the objectives of your marketing plan. For example, if an objective in your marketing plan is to increase sales during weekday dinners by 20 percent in the next year, then your promotion plan objectives should focus on achieving that goal. Promotion objectives that support this marketing plan objective might include training the dinner servers on **suggestive selling**—suggesting additional items to people who are buying something; distributing a press release about special dinner menu items; developing a sales promotion to increase customer traffic during weekday dinners; or creating an advertising campaign to bring in new customers during weekday dinners.

When developing objectives for your promotion plan, think about:

- **Both short-term and long-term objectives of your plan**—What can you do right away to begin meeting the long-term objectives in your marketing plan? For example, a short-term objective for a promotion might be highlighting a new entrée, while a long-term objective might be building a new customer base.

- **Return on your promotion investment**—What value do you want to get for the money you spend on the promotion? In some cases, breaking even might be worth it because the potential long-term benefits would outweigh the cost.

Since promotional objectives need to be measurable, it makes sense to develop mechanisms for tracking the promotional results while you are developing the objectives. Defining these mechanisms before you implement your plan helps you recognize certain milestones of success or failure after the promotion starts. For example, you might want to see a specific number of patrons using a coupon during different day parts, or you might want to see a certain amount of increased revenue directly associated with a promotion. Tracking the results also helps you to know whether a promotion is meeting the objectives you set both for the promotion and for your marketing plan.

Exhibit 5e

Elements of a Promotion Mix

Newspaper advertisement

Carry-out menu

Gift card

A consistent message improves the chances of success.

Determining the Message Strategy

At some point while developing your promotional plan, usually after you set your objectives, you need to decide at a high level the message you want your promotion mix to communicate to customers. It is important to think about your message before you determine your promotion mix because, to be most effective, your message needs to be integrated throughout all your promotions.

Your promotions communicate not only through the words they use, but also through the message format and structure. Together, these components form your message and communicate an image of your restaurant.

When determining a message strategy:

- **Use similar words, format, and structure in all parts of your promotion mix.** (See *Exhibit 5e.*) This consistency helps to create a clear message, which increases its chances of getting through to the right people.

- **Integrate your target audience's needs.** For example, if your target audience is health conscious, plan to integrate nutritional information into your message, and make nutritional information available through your promotion materials. Use your value proposition as a foundation.

- **Make your message unique and specific.** Do not duplicate what your competitors are doing. For instance, suppose five restaurants in your competitive set—your primary group of competitors—are using a percentage-off meal coupon. If you use a similar promotion, a customer would not have a compelling reason to patronize your establishment over the other restaurants.

- **Use promotion materials that convey the appropriate image.** Not all promotions are appropriate for all types of restaurants. For example, door-hanger menus would not be consistent with the image that a fine-dining restaurant would want to convey.

After you have decided on a strategy for your promotions, you are ready to begin choosing your promotion tactics and how to implement your strategy. This involves selecting your promotion mix and then planning the details of each part of your mix.

Selecting Your Promotion Mix

Different parts of the promotion mix offer different advantages and disadvantages, as summarized in *Exhibit 5f*. Your promotion strategies, which are based on your marketing plan, should drive the combination of components in the promotion mix. Each of these components is explained in more detail in the following sections.

Exhibit 5f

Pros and Cons of Promotion Mix Components

Component	Pros	Cons
Advertising	■ Able to reach a wide audience ■ Targets multiple media vehicles	■ May be costly ■ Is nonpersonal ■ Requires repeated exposures to be effective
Sales promotions	■ Able to be creative ■ Can generate immediate sales	■ May be costly ■ May be time-consuming
Public relations	■ Involves the restaurant within the community ■ Perceived as more credible than other types of promotions ■ Publicity is free	■ Risk of bad publicity ■ Lack of control ■ May be time-consuming ■ Can be costly if paying for public relations firm or consultant
Personal selling	■ Provides the seller with instant feedback ■ Builds relationships with customers	■ Is costly when dedicated sales staff are used

Using Advertising

Advertising is often the most visible part of a company's promotion mix and can reach a wide audience. A well-planned **advertising campaign** is a coordinated series of advertisements and other promotions used in the same time frame to meet certain objectives. It offers many benefits, including:

- Generating awareness of and interest in a product or service

- Persuading the audience to take action, such as purchasing a product

- Strengthening existing customer preferences and loyalty

■ Creating or reinforcing an image of a product or organization

■ Differentiating a restaurant's products and services from its competitors

■ Communicating a message to a large audience

■ Reaching a target audience through multiple media when used, such as radio, print, and television

Advertising is often used to create awareness of other parts of the promotion mix, particularly sales promotions and public relations events. For example, a restaurant might use advertisements to promote and distribute coupons or to create awareness of a charity event it is hosting.

Exhibit 5g

Summary of Advertising Disadvantages and Ways to Deal with Them

Disadvantage	Counteraction
Advertising is impersonal.	Personalize the advertisement.
Advertising must compete for customer attention.	Make your ad stand out.
Advertising is costly.	Look for cost-saving opportunities, such as cooperative advertising.

Given the benefits of advertising, you might think that all restaurants should include advertising in their promotion mix. However, advertising also has disadvantages, and it is not always the best choice for every situation. Before you integrate advertising into your restaurant's promotion mix, you need to understand the disadvantages of advertising and what you can do to counteract them. (See *Exhibit 5g*.)

Advertising may be seen as impersonal and therefore is not as persuasive as an individual in a sales capacity. To counteract this, introduce elements to personalize your advertisements. Are there opportunities to present the management or staff within the advertising? Can the image portrayed by the restaurant be more personal? By making advertising more personal, the public will make a personal connection to the restaurant and will be more likely to remember the advertisement.

Advertising also must compete for attention. The public is selective in what it will respond or pay attention to since it is bombarded with advertising through multiple media on a daily basis. As a consequence, the most effective ads stand out from the others. Having an ad stand out may mean using a less traditional type of media, such as an Internet banner ad, or using an innovative idea or motto.

Finally, advertising can be costly. Depending on the media used, the production quality of the ad, and the amount of exposure you purchase for the advertising, the costs can vary dramatically.

For example, the cost of producing a television commercial and airing it in a large, urban market will be very high compared to the cost of creating a small print ad and running it in a college newspaper. However, when considering the costs of advertising, keep these things in mind:

■ The value of running an advertisement is based not only on its cost but also on its cost per **exposure,** defined by the American Marketing Association as "any opportunity for a reader, viewer, or listener to see and/or hear an advertising message in a particular media vehicle." A **media vehicle** is a particular television channel, newspaper, magazine, Web site, or other specific media channel.

■ Advertising is part of a long-term investment in the success of your restaurant. Normally, people need to be exposed to an ad several times before they notice and remember it. Therefore, it may take weeks, months, or even years of advertising and marketing efforts to bring in some customers.

Given the costs and characteristics of advertising, it is essential to choose the right advertising media for your restaurant.

Choosing Your Media

The media you choose for your advertising and other promotions can make or break your marketing plan. As with all marketing activities, your choices of media should be based on your target audience and your objectives. Furthermore, there are several criteria you must consider when choosing media:

■ **Frequency**—How often and how many times should your target audience be exposed to your restaurant's advertisements?

■ **Media type**—Which media type (television, radio, Internet, etc.) is the best for conveying your message?

■ **Reach**—How effectively will various media vehicles reach your target audience?

■ **Scheduling**—When is the most effective time to run your advertisements?

Each of these criteria is discussed in more detail in the following sections.

Frequency and Reach

Estimating how often and how many times a target audience should be exposed to an advertisement can be a challenging task. Although there are various theories about how many times an advertisement

---

Think About It…

According to Nielsen Media Research, the average child viewed 1,265 restaurant commercials in 2003.

must be seen or heard before it registers with a target audience, in general, the more times someone is exposed to an advertisement, the better the chances that he or she will notice it.

To determine how well a media vehicle can reach your target audience, you need to analyze how many people are in that vehicle's audience and their demographics and segmentation. For example, suppose you are considering using a local entertainment newspaper for your advertisements. Before you purchase ad space, you need to know how many people from your target audience read that newspaper.

Reach is commonly expressed as a percentage of the number of people from your target market who are in the media vehicle's audience.

$$\frac{\text{Number of people the media vehicle reaches from your target audience}}{\text{Total number of people in the media vehicle audience}} \times 100\% = \text{Reach}$$

For instance, suppose your target audience is middle-income people from thirty-five to fifty years old. You are considering advertising in a newspaper with a total audience of 100,000 people. (To get audience information for a specific media vehicle, talk to one of its sales representatives.) If 40,000 of these readers are middle-income and between thirty-five to fifty years old, then the newspaper's reach is 40 percent. When you purchase an ad, you are paying for all the exposure provided by a media vehicle, so the remaining exposure is a waste of money (in this case, the remaining 60 percent of the newspaper's reach). However, the value for you is in the cost per exposure to your target audience. Using this example, if the ad costs $1,000, your cost per exposure is 2.5 cents per exposure:

$$\frac{\$1,000 \text{ ad cost}}{40,000 \text{ exposures}} = \$0.025 \text{ per exposure}$$

Media Types

Different media offer different advantages and disadvantages, as *Exhibit 5h* on the next page shows. When choosing a media type, consider these factors and how effectively a specific media type can convey your message. For example, if you want to advertise a promotion that involves coupons, you must use a media type that can provide customers with coupons, such as newspapers, magazines, direct mail, or the Internet. Or, if you want to highlight the expertise of your chefs, you might use a television ad to show the chefs at work and the appetizing meals they produce.

Exhibit 5h

Media Type Pros and Cons

Media Type	Pros	Cons
Television	■ Can target specific markets ■ Can reach a large population ■ Provides video and audio ■ Specific timing of ads	■ Usually expensive ■ Limited time for conveying message ■ Technology exists that enables viewers to avoid commercials ■ Transitory; cannot look at again
Radio	■ Low cost ■ Can target specific markets ■ May reach a relatively large population ■ Specific timing of ads	■ No visuals ■ Limited time for conveying message ■ Transitory; cannot listen to again
Newspaper	■ Can target a local area ■ Usually inexpensive compared to other media ■ Short lead time for ads	■ High level of competition with other ads ■ Short life span; usually discarded daily ■ Low production quality
Internet	■ Can target specific markets ■ Can use limited video and audio ■ Can be interactive (e.g., print coupons, find a location) ■ Timing is controlled by the audience	■ May be costly ■ More difficult to accurately target audiences
Magazine	■ Can target very specific markets ■ Long life span ■ High quality production	■ Long lead time for ads ■ Usually most costly print media
Direct mail	■ Can target very specific markets ■ Great control over content	■ Requires accurate, timely data ■ Easy to be ignored ■ High cost per exposure ■ Negative image
Outdoor advertising	■ Provides high exposure rates ■ Low cost per exposure for broad target audiences ■ Good for targeting an audience by location	■ Not good for targeting small markets ■ Sometimes limited by local regulations ■ Long lead time for ads

Scheduling

Although your promotion plan should specify some elements of your schedule, such as the start and end times for the promotion, you still must choose the best days and times within that range to ensure that your message reaches your target audience. The scheduling strategy you use should be based on your objectives and research. For example, if you want to increase party bookings during the holiday season, you need to know when people are most likely to be planning these parties, and then form a scheduling strategy based on this information.

Once you have identified a date range for your promotion plan, you can determine a scheduling strategy within those dates. This strategy should address:

- **Patterns of advertising**—You can run advertising on a consistent basis, such as one ad per week for three months; in intermittent bursts, such as several ads just before certain holidays or seasonal slow periods; or in a combination of the two methods, such as two ads per month, with bursts of advertising just before the holidays.

- **Best times to communicate your message to your target audience**—For example, if your promotional message is that your restaurant is a great place to pick up a family dinner, you might want to buy radio ads that are broadcast during the evening rush hour. Or, if your message is that your restaurant is a romantic place for a special occasion, you might run newspaper or magazine ads before Valentine's Day, Mother's Day, or New Year's Eve.

Crafting Your Message

To be successful, your advertising must communicate effectively. If your message is unclear or poorly presented, customers will not receive the message you intended. A common model for creating advertising messages is **AIDA:**

- **Attention**—Get the audience's attention.

- **Interest**—Interest the audience in your message.

- **Desire**—Create a desire for your product.

- **Action**—Prompt the audience to take the desired action.

In addition, you need to consider several other factors:

- **Promotional messages of your competitors**—A successful promotion is one that is unique and specific. Monitor your competitors' promotions, and avoid duplicating what they are doing.

- **Regulations regarding truth in advertising**—Understand what you can and cannot say or portray. The Federal Trade Commission (FTC) specifies that "advertising must be truthful and nondeceptive; advertisers must have evidence to back up their claims; and advertisements cannot be unfair." If you are making claims related to nutrition, you also need to understand what can be categorized as "healthy." In addition, you should be familiar with any state and local regulations.

- **Optimum use of the media type**—Each medium has things it does well and things it cannot do or does poorly. How can you take advantage of the media type? If you are using the Internet, for example, you might provide links to download your menu and to show your location through a mapping service.

- **Image you want to convey for your restaurant**—Your message should align with your restaurant concept; for example, a quick-service restaurant and a fine-dining restaurant need to convey very different images. Your use of media, color, music, and materials all affect customers' perception of your restaurant and message.

Activity

Identifying Images

Look at each of the ads shown below, and describe the type of restaurant you think each ad represents. Discuss your responses with your classmates.

When you are *hungry* and in a *hurry*, come to

Sandwich Sally's

**Where *hot* sandwiches are *hot*,
cold sandwiches are *cold*,
and *all* sandwiches are GREAT!**

✗ Ask about our daily specials: soup, salad, & cookie!
✗ Eat inside or use our convenient drive-thru.
✗ Intersection of Hwy 83 and Washington Street.
✗ Phone ahead for quicker service: 830-555-2137
✗ Or fax in your order for pickup: 830–555-2246

For the *finest* in *French haute cuisine*—

Chateau Magnifique

This week we are featuring the area's finest
Chateaubriand accompanied by our sommelier's
selection from our extensive wine cellar.
Of course, all our standard fare is also available
for your dining pleasure.

Chateau Magnifique. Need we say more?

110 Empire Boulevard
Reservations required. 312-555-0100

Why not take the entire family out for dinner
and give your cook a rest?
The perfect place for good home cooking & lots of it is

Grandma Gertie's

Food the way your grandma used to make,
including meatloaf and mashed potatoes,
Southern fried chicken, and chicken-fried steak.
Fresh soup made daily.
Special menu for children under 12.

Just come on down no reservations required.
2744 S. Parkway, near the Interstate entrance.
Phone ahead for quicker service: 916-555-3379
Or fax in your order for pickup: 916-555-3444

Using Public Relations

The purpose of public relations—the next part of the promotion mix—is to generate publicity. The main benefit of publicity is that people find it more believable than advertising. If you read a glowing review of a restaurant in a company newsletter, for example, you would be more prone to go there than you if you just saw a newspaper ad for the restaurant. However, while positive publicity is a great advantage, negative publicity can damage the credibility of your establishment. The main disadvantage of publicity is that you have no control over it. If your restaurant receives negative publicity (for example, a bad review), you may need to use other portions of your promotion mix for damage control.

As a restaurant professional, there are two main areas that you should focus on to incorporate public relations in your promotion mix: media relations and community relations.

Community Relations

Community relations involve interacting with the people in your local area to create awareness of and trust for your business. Activities such as hosting charity events, giving tours, and sponsoring sports teams are examples of community relations. These types of activities are a way to "give back" to the community. They also provide many benefits for both a restaurant and its managers, such as:

- Creating a positive image within the community

- Building credibility within the community

- Building relationships with other community leaders

- Creating a network with other restaurant professionals

- Generating positive publicity

- Promoting the restaurant

The opportunities for building good community relations are as limitless as your imagination. One way is to support a local community group with donations of volunteer work, money, food, or meeting space. For example, donating a portion of sales from a certain promotion or offering discounts for customers who donate to a chosen charity helps to build your reputation within the community and promote customer patronage. *Exhibit 5i* on the next page shows various types of organizations that your restaurant (or you personally) could support. Another way to get involved is to participate in community events, such as festivals, fairs, and parades.

Think About It...

To offset a bad review, consider an advertising campaign with testimonials from well-known local celebrities who frequent your restaurant.

Exhibit 5i

Types of Organizations Offering Community Relations Opportunities

- Schools and student organizations, such as:
  - ☐ Sports teams
  - ☐ Clubs
  - ☐ Music programs
- Business organizations
- State and local chambers of commerce
- Community organizations and clubs, such as:
  - ☐ Youth groups
  - ☐ Women's centers
  - ☐ Men's centers
  - ☐ Senior citizen centers
  - ☐ Student organizations
- Ecology and conservation organizations
- Animal welfare organizations
- Welcoming organizations
- YMCAs and YWCAs
- Local sports leagues
- Rotary clubs, Lions clubs, Kiwanis, and other service organizations
- Convention and visitors bureaus

- Not-for-profit social service organizations, such as:
  - ☐ Literacy-related organizations
  - ☐ Job placement centers in human service organizations
  - ☐ Homeless shelters
  - ☐ Food banks
- Churches, synagogues, mosques, and other religious institutions
- Local hospitality-oriented professional organizations, such as:
  - ☐ Local chapters of the National Restaurant Association
  - ☐ Local hospitality and lodging associations
  - ☐ Les Amis du Vin
  - ☐ Les Dames d'Escoffier
  - ☐ Local chapters of the American Culinary Federation
  - ☐ The Federation of Dining Room Professionals
  - ☐ Confrérie de la Chaîne des Rôtisseurs

Any level of community involvement on behalf of your restaurant will help to make others more aware of your business. For example, even if you are the only person from your restaurant that becomes involved in an organization, people who get to know you from that organization will start noticing your restaurant. The more involved you and your employees become in the community, the more awareness you generate.

The cost of becoming involved in organizations and events can vary. You may need to pay yearly dues or meeting fees to be involved with some organizations, but you probably will not need to pay anything to volunteer at other organizations, such as a local homeless shelter. If you choose to support an organization with donations of food, labor, money, or space, some of these costs may be tax-deductible. (Make sure to check with your tax advisor.) However, you should view any costs you incur as an investment in both your community and your restaurant.

Choosing the Right Organization or Event

Since community relations activities involve some level of commitment on your part, and since public relations activities should be geared toward your target market just as any other part of your promotion mix, you should identify which organizations or events best fit with your marketing plan. Before you invest a great deal of time or money in an organization or community event, consider how well this involvement may support your marketing plan.

- Do you believe in the cause of the organization or event? Do its goals and philosophies align with the image of your restaurant?

- Do its members or participants belong to your target market or have influence with your target market?

- What kind of opportunities does it present for publicity in your target market?

- What kind of support can you provide? Will this level of support make enough of a difference to generate good publicity?

If your target market is families, for instance, you might become involved with supporting school activities or youth sports teams. Or, if your target market is business professionals, you might become involved with business organizations or charities that are supported by businesses in your market area.

Developing Programs to Generate Publicity

Once you have identified community relations opportunities that align with your marketing plan, you can begin thinking about how to become involved in a way that generates good publicity. (See *Exhibit 5j.*) For example, you can develop promotions or sales that support your chosen organization or event while generating business for your restaurant, such as:

- Offering discounts to schoolchildren who get good grades or attendance

- Donating a portion of sales to charity for a given item, day part, or day

- Offering customers a discount when they bring in a donation for charity

- Sponsoring a local children's sports team and offering incentives for winning a game

- Offering your facility or providing the catering for a fundraiser or meeting

Exhibit 5j

Giving back to the community can generate good publicity.

Other types of programs may not generate direct business but can still provide excellent opportunities for publicity. For example, consider the publicity that might be generated if your restaurant donates food, labor, or equipment to a soup kitchen.

Good publicity usually does not happen on its own. The best way to ensure good publicity is by building good relationships with the media and communicating your activities to them.

Media Relations

While you may not be able to control the publicity about your restaurant, you can have a positive effect if you know what and how to communicate to the media. Ideally, you also should develop a professional relationship with media representatives. These actions—providing publicity materials to the media and working with media representatives—are known as **media relations.**

Good media relations can exponentially increase the impact of your community relations programs. For example, suppose you create a special promotion to discount meals for people who donate to the local food bank. If you promote this discount on your own or with the help of the food bank, it is likely that the only people who will know about the discount will be those in the target markets of your restaurant or the food bank. On the other hand, if you have good media relations and can generate a story in the local media, you can reach many more people—people who will be more likely to notice your good work and respond in a positive way.

To get the best return on your community relations investments, you should coordinate your community relations and media relations programs. Part of this involves choosing the right media vehicles.

Choosing the Right Media Vehicles

With any form of marketing communications, you need to focus your efforts on reaching your target market. When evaluating potential types of media and media vehicles, such as particular publications or radio stations, consider the following questions:

- Does the media vehicle reach your target market or people who can influence your target market? If so, how much of your target market does it reach? Use the same criteria to evaluate the media vehicle as you would for an advertising campaign.

- How likely is it that the media vehicle will be interested in the stories you submit? Do you have a story that may interest its audience members?

- Have you established a good relationship or history with any media representatives? If not, how easily can you develop these relationships?

- Can your public relations materials effectively compete for attention from the decision makers in this media vehicle? If not, can you improve your materials to make them more competitive?

These last two points are interrelated. If you have a good relationship with a newspaper editor, for example, your materials are more likely to get the editor's attention. Likewise, if you understand what gets the editor's attention in the first place—if you send effective public relations materials— you are more likely to develop a good working relationship with that editor.

Using Effective Public Relations Materials

To directly generate publicity through the media, businesses commonly send out press releases and/or media kits. A **press release** or **news release** is a brief presentation of promotional information written in a general and timely news format. Well-written press releases present marketing information as news. (See *Exhibit 5k*.) If a business is lucky, the information in its press release will be published or read "as is," but more often, the information will be incorporated into a story. A press release may be sent by itself or as part of a press kit.

Exhibit 5k

Sample Press Release

THREE LANDS RESTAURANT
141 Lincoln Drive, Minneapolis, Minnesota, 55401
Tel. (612) 555-1200 Fax: (612) 555-1239
WWW.THREELANDS.COM

FOR IMMEDIATE RELEASE
Contact:
Pat Park
Three Lands Restaurant
(612) 555-1200
ppark@threelands.com

Three Lands Restaurant Raises Funds for Disaster Relief

MINNEAPOLIS (July 6, 2007)—To help people around the world who have recently experienced a major disaster, the Three Lands Restaurant will donate 25 percent of all revenue collected during its weeklong Summer Fling event starting July 19 to the International Red Cross. Three Lands' Summer Fling is an outdoor event featuring special, grilled menu items and live entertainment.

"We are excited that we can help the Red Cross help so many people while providing a special celebration of the season," says Three Lands General Manager Terry Larsen. "Since so many disasters have occurred recently, we are especially glad to support such a worthy organization as the Red Cross."

Supporters who come to Three Lands' Summer Fling can expect to find a special menu featuring juicy, grilled burgers, chicken, and chorizo; locally grown, grilled sweet corn with chili-lime butter; ceviché salade Niçoise with cilantro vinaigrette; and of course, Three Lands' famous tropical drinks and wide selection of imported beers and wine. Chef-owner Javier Diaz also is offering special dessert items, including guava crème brûlée, tropical fruit snow cones, horchata frozen custard, and chocolate tamales.

Each night of the Summer Fling presents a different local band, including the Motion Poets, Slide Huxtable, The Righteous, and Little Big. Saturday and Sunday, the music starts at noon. For a complete schedule, check the restaurant's Web site at www.threelands.com.

Red Cross regional director, Connie Puntillo, states, "This type of event brings the community together to help others who really need it. We are so grateful for the help and donations of people like Javier and his staff. I hope everyone turns out to support this event."

Founded in 1998 by chef-owner Javier Diaz,
Three Lands Restaurant offers a blend of cuisines from North America, South America, and Europe.
Its award-winning menu has been recognized nationwide for its creativity.

A **press kit,** also called a **media kit,** is a packet of information given to media representatives to answer questions they might have about a business or organization. (Press kits also may be given to prospective customers, employees, or investors.) Some restaurants also provide their press kits in an electronic format, often through a Web site or CD-ROM. Typically, a press kit for a restaurant is a folder that contains:

■ General information about the restaurant

■ Menus

■ Any recent articles or press releases

■ List of any recent awards

■ Photos of the establishment and its menu items

■ The restaurant's mission or goal statement

■ Contact information for the restaurant spokesperson

■ Other promotional materials

The key to the press kit, like any other type of marketing communication, is to get noticed so that the restaurant, in turn, gets noticed. As a restaurant manager, you should do what you believe is necessary in terms of quality and creativity to ensure that your operation's press kit gets noticed.

Activity

Investigating Online Media Relations

Visit the Web sites of at least three restaurants or restaurant companies to learn how they handle media relations through the Internet. For each company, record the restaurant name and Web site address (URL), and then answer the following questions. Be prepared to discuss your answers in class.

1 How easy was it to determine whether the site contained information intended for media representatives? Did the home page contain a link called "Media Relations," "Press," or something similar?

2 Did the site contain an online or "virtual" press kit?

☐ If so, what information was in the press kit? How was the information presented? Did the site offer an option for downloading the press kit?

☐ If not, did the site contain information you would expect to find in a press kit, such as facts about the restaurant, press releases, and articles?

3 Did the site provide information on how to contact a spokesperson for more information about the company or to receive a hard copy of a press kit?

4 Suppose you are a reporter writing a story about restaurants. Which site did you like the best, which site did you like the least, and why?

Using Sales Promotions

Sales promotions, another part of the promotion mix, provide special incentives for customers to patronize your restaurant. There are many types of sales promotions and different tools or materials that can be used in a sales promotion. All are designed to give your customers that extra "boost" to get them into your restaurant or to purchase certain items. However, sales promotions are only useful when your customers know about them, which is why they are often the focus of a restaurant's advertising.

As with any part of the promotion mix, sales promotions need to support your marketing plan, your product positioning, and your restaurant's image. Therefore, you need to carefully consider your choices in sales promotion methods and materials.

Sales Promotion Methods

There are many types of sales promotion methods you can use in your promotion mix. Each offers customers a certain incentive, as shown in *Exhibit 5l*. Each promotion type also has advantages and disadvantages, as discussed in the following sections.

Exhibit 5l

Types of Sales Promotions

Method	Description	Incentive to the Customer
Special pricing	Limited-time reduced prices implemented through specials, deals, coupons, or other programs	■ Savings on an item ■ Low-risk opportunity to try a new item
Frequent shopper programs	Gives a benefit in exchange for continuing patronage	Rewards for continued patronage (usually free meals)
Premiums	Free or reduced-price merchandise that may or may not show the name and location of the restaurant, usually given away or sold for a reduced price with the purchase of a food item	Free or reduced-price merchandise
Special events	One-time or periodic occasions that provide a special incentive for the customer to patronize your restaurant	Varies based on event
Samples	Free, small taste of food items	Risk-free opportunity to try a new item
Contests and sweepstakes	Games and other programs that involve the customer and provide a prize	Chance to win a product or service

Special Pricing

Sales promotions that involve reduced prices for a specific or limited time are one of the most common ways for businesses to promote their products. This method allows customers to try a product at a reduced cost. For restaurants, special pricing programs include such things as:

■ **Deals** or **specials**—Short-term price reductions on a certain product for a specific period of time. Restaurant deals or specials often consist of a free meal course with the purchase of a select entrée. For example, a restaurant may offer a free piece of pie with the purchase of a meatloaf dinner.

■ **Coupons**—Certificates designed to entice the customer to try a restaurant or an item, usually by offering a discounted price. The function of coupons is to stimulate demand for a particular item or during a particular period. Coupons are also useful for promoting the trial of a new product.

Exhibit 5m

Special pricing offers customers a way to try items for less money.

Deals and specials are typically communicated within the establishment through servers, menu boards, and table tentcards. Outside the operation, these types of promotions may be communicated through signage, advertisements, and other materials, as shown in *Exhibit 5m*. Coupons are often included in advertisements, takeout menus, and flyers.

Coupons offer a huge benefit that most other promotions cannot offer as easily: traceability. If you run an advertisement with a coupon in two newspapers, for example, you can put a different code on each coupon. As the coupons are redeemed, you can see which newspaper ad brought in more business. Large, multiunit operations in particular may use **clearinghouses,** departments or third-party firms that specialize in processing coupons and providing other marketing assistance to track coupon origins and patterns of use.

The use of special pricing programs may not always be a good choice. The overuse of discounts—deals, specials, and coupons—can backfire by creating the customer perception that certain items are not worth the full price. In addition, these types of programs may not be consistent with the image you want to portray for your restaurant. As with any type of marketing effort, you need to carefully consider how your promotion will affect your customers' short-term and long-term spending habits and your restaurant's bottom line.

For example, a classic case of oversaturating a market with coupons happened in the pizza industry. Various pizzerias started distributing coupons to households on a weekly basis. Since every restaurant was distributing coupons, it made it harder for any one establishment to stand out in the crowd. To counter this problem, several shops decided to also honor their competitors' coupons. This promotion resulted in deep discounts that the restaurants had to honor since they had advertised that they would accept any competitor's coupon. Ultimately, this promotion severly cut into the pizzerias' profit.

If you are considering using a promotion that involves special pricing or discounts, you need to compare its potential costs and benefits. If you are using coupons, you also need to consider the time and costs associated with delivering and processing the actual coupons as part of your expenses. These costs may vary greatly based on the size and type of your operation. Franchise establishments may split the costs of coupons with their corporate office.

Frequent Diner Programs

A promotion method used primarily to increase customer loyalty, **frequent diner programs,** or **reward programs,** provide an incentive to customers who purchase a set number of meals or items or visit a restaurant a set number of times. These programs are similar to the frequent flyer programs used by airlines. For example, a customer may receive a free sandwich after purchasing ten sandwiches over the course of several visits. Typically, frequent diner programs differ from deals or specials in that they require repeated visits to receive the reward. Sometimes, the programs can have time limits, such as having to purchase ten sandwiches within one year to receive a free sandwich.

Restaurants that use frequent diner programs often distribute cards to track the number of items a customer has purchased. Customers who use these cards often return to the restaurants that sponsor them, so they can build up points. This repeat business creates customer loyalty.

As with samples, you must clearly examine the implementation and cost of this type of promotion. For example, employees must be trained to follow the program rules, so that they do not give away food or food credits unless the customer actually purchases the required items or makes the required number of visits.

Exhibit 5n

Premiums provide
incentives for
purchasing a product.

Premiums

Another type of promotion involves the use of premiums. **Premiums** are merchandise offered to customers for free or for a low price as an incentive to purchase a product. For example, during the holiday season, quick-service chains may offer a holiday toy, figurine, or glass for free or at a discounted price with the purchase of a specific meal. (See *Exhibit 5n.*) Premiums encourage customers to buy more of a particular product or to return more often to a restaurant, such as to collect a set of glasses.

Like other promotions, premiums offer both advantages and disadvantages. If they are popular, premiums can bring in a large number of customers. However, if customers are only buying your product to get the premium, the promotion will have a short-term effect, and your promotion dollars could have been better spent in other ways.

In addition, premiums can be expensive, depending on how much they cost and how much, if anything, you charge for them. They usually have a limited lifespan; for example, a restaurant may offer premiums related to a sporting event or movie. You need to be especially careful when purchasing premiums that have a limited lifespan; you do not want to purchase more premiums than you need, but if you purchase too few, you risk alienating customers who come in for the premium.

Special Events

Special events are one-time or periodic occasions that provide a special incentive for customers to patronize your restaurant. The most effective special-event promotions provide a "hook" to entice your customers to make a special visit to your restaurant. For example, you might plan wine tastings, restaurant tours, or other informational events. Other types of special events include special menus related to popular seasonal ingredients, such as seafood or local produce, and festivals related to seasonal or other themes, such as Oktoberfest, a jazz festival, or a family day.

Special events can provide a great vehicle for generating publicity, especially if you cosponsor the event with other organizations and promote the event using other elements of your promotion mix. However, special events take a lot of planning and require a great deal of organization. For example, if your restaurant has an outdoor music festival, you will need to coordinate the entertainment, the stage and equipment, and the extra staffing, among other things. Special events also can be expensive, but the potential benefits should determine whether or not you go ahead with an event.

Samples

Another type of promotion, which customers view as risk-free, is the sample. **Samples** are small amounts of product offered free to customers to give them the chance to try a certain product or dish. For example, bakeries often offer a sample tray of pastries they are trying to promote. Samples often induce an immediate purchase, allowing the restaurant to quickly sell an item.

Depending on the portion of the sample, the product, and its distribution, samples may be costly or provide a poor return on investment. For example, if a restaurant offers samples of an expensive item such as lobster, the restaurant may risk losing money if the sample sizes are too big. Similarly, if employees are not trained to ensure that customers do not take unfair advantage of a sample offer, a limited number of customers may consume all the samples intended for a larger group.

Finally, to ensure the best return on this type of investment, the sample quality must be as high-quality as anything else being sold in the establishment. Ensuring that samples are fresh is critical for both sanitation and quality issues.

Contests and Sweepstakes

Contests and sweepstakes provide customers with opportunities to receive a special product or service. Unlike other types of sales promotions, these programs require that customers actively participate, and the rewards given to customers may range from a discounted or free food item to an expensive prize, such as a car or cash. Contests and sweepstakes can provide a great reason for businesses to conduct new advertising campaigns. They also provide a good way to collect customer information for your marketing information system.

In a **contest,** the customer is asked to submit an idea, such as a slogan for a new product, answer a question, or demonstrate a skill. Contests encourage customers to become involved with an organization. However, the time and effort to set up a contest is often costly, and the contest must be examined for its practicality to the organization.

Sweepstakes are games of chance. Usually, they only require customers to submit their name and contact information. A common type of sweepstakes in some restaurants is a drawing for a free meal or other incentive. Often, these restaurants place a bowl at the entrance and ask customers to drop in their business card for a chance to win a prize.

With any contest or sweepstakes, you should define the rules very clearly so both customers and employees understand them. In addition, you should seek legal advice before implementing any contest or sweepstakes program.

Promotion Materials

Some sales promotion methods use materials such as coupons for special pricing programs or toys for premiums. However, other promotion materials support your marketing plan by continuously promoting your restaurant even when you are not running an active promotion program. **Promotion materials** are miscellaneous items that do not necessarily offer incentives for visiting your restaurant, but they increase awareness of your establishment. (See *Exhibit 5o*.) A menu board placed outside your establishment is an example of promotion materials. While some of these materials do not offer the customer any true benefit, they present the restaurant's information in places where customers can notice it.

Exhibit 5o

Typical Promotional Materials

Promotional Material	Description
Signage	Menu boards, directional signs, and other signs that indicate where the restaurant is located and/or items served
Flyers	Paper notices that are randomly distributed or targeted to a specific group to create awareness of a certain promotion or menu item
Trinkets	Token gifts or "give-away" items, such as matchbooks, pens, or stationary, that display the restaurant name and location or phone number
Carry-out and door hanger menus	Paper menu for customers to use outside of the restaurant; door hanger menus for hanging on doorknobs or handles
Apparel	Your restaurant name and/or logo on a t-shirt or other garment
Point of purchase (POP) materials	Menu boards, video, print pieces, and other display items near the **point of purchase**—where customers pay for their purchases
Merchandising materials	Table tents and other display items in the restaurant

Using Personal Selling

Another component of the promotion mix, personal selling, allows the manager, salesperson, or server to receive immediate feedback from the customer. Personal selling also allows the sales staff to explain the benefits of the restaurant in detail and answer any immediate questions from the customer. While the feedback from other areas of the promotion mix is relatively slow, in personal selling, you know almost immediately if the customer will purchase anything.

In a restaurant, many people may be involved in personal selling. Servers usually have the most contact with customers and, therefore, the most opportunities for personal selling. Ideally, though, everyone in the operation should be involved. Those who have direct contact with customers should be continuously looking for personal selling opportunities. For example, if a hostess notices a customer eyeing a pie display, she should use the opportunity to try to sell the customer a pie. However, in some restaurants, particularly large operations that offer private rooms, banquet facilities, and catering services, there also may be a designated person or team whose main responsibility is to market or sell the restaurant's concept and services.

Personal Selling by Designated Salespeople

In operations that have designated salespeople, a sales team might work one-on-one with clients or groups to sell specialized dinners or large spaces for an event. This type of selling also happens in smaller establishments, but it usually is done by the manager or owner instead of a sales team.

This type of personal selling is expensive. When using it in your promotion mix, you should be fully aware of the costs associated with selling and the salaries and commissions given to the sales staff. **Commissions** are a percentage of the selling price given as a payment to staff members who sell your products and services. There may be different percentages for different amounts sold in a time period, and there may be a minimum amount sold—called a **sales quota** or sales objective—that must be met to receive any commission. In addition to the salaries and commissions, there is the added cost of maintaining your sales efforts. Travel expenses, meals, and office supplies all add up in the cost structure of this type of personal selling. While smaller restaurants might not use the same structures, they too will incur some of these expenses with a sales staff.

Personal Selling by Staff

Personal selling is also widely found at the staff level within restaurants. As discussed before, keeping your staff fully informed of promotion details enables them to tell customers about a particular promotion. Staff who use this selling technique are able to quickly market and sell items on the menu during a customer interaction. For example, a server may offer a customer wine and suggest wine selections without being asked. For customers who may not have considered wine, this is an excellent reminder.

Many restaurants offer incentives for the staff to perform this personal selling. They may hold daily contests to see how many servers can sell a particular entrée or special of the evening and reward them financially or with a prize. In addition, since the majority of servers are also paid a gratuity, it benefits them to sell items that increase a customer's check.

Networking as a Tool

While most personal selling opportunities are created through the workplace, some may occur away from the job. As a restaurant manager, you should be looking for these opportunities and encouraging your employees to do so as well. One way to do this is by actively networking with the people you meet in your community. Networking is the practice of building and maintaining ongoing communication with individuals you can help and who can also help you. Good networking produces good publicity and can generate sales leads. (It is also a great way to find new employees.)

To build a network, you might want to join the local chamber of commerce or a convention and visitors bureau to begin building a network with other individuals in or outside the restaurant field. Or, you might consider becoming active in trade or professional organizations in your area.

You can enhance your networking relationships by offering coupons or discount cards to people you meet. These promotions encourage people to visit your establishment. Also give these tools to your employees, and instruct them on when to use them.

Using Cooperative Marketing

Within your promotion mix, there may be opportunities for cooperative marketing—marketing activities that are shared by two or more business firms, nonprofit organizations, government agencies, or individuals. Common types of cooperative marketing include:

- Cooperative sales promotions—When two or more sponsors develop complementary promotions or offer complementary promotion materials. (See *Exhibit 5p.*) For example, a restaurant hands out coupons for free admission to a sports event, and the sports team hands out coupons for a free appetizer at the restaurant.

- Cooperative advertising—When two or more sponsors share the cost of an advertisement or advertising campaign. For example, a neighboring restaurant and hotel might develop an advertising campaign to attract new business, or several businesses might pool

Exhibit 5p

Example of Cooperative Advertising

their marketing resources to advertise a common festival or event.

A related practice is the use of **trade-outs** or **bartering,** when goods or services are exchanged in lieu of money. In restaurant marketing, trade-outs are most common when a restaurant provides free services to the office of a media vehicle, such as a newspaper, radio station, or television station, in exchange for a "plug" or publicity.

Of course, even though cooperative marketing can stretch your marketing dollar, you still should ensure these types of promotions will support your marketing plan.

Planning the Implementation

Building your business is easier said than done. Implementing frequent activities and promotions are difficult to execute if you are not organized. One way to stay organized is to develop a simple checklist that answers the following questions:

- Who is responsible for the overall event or promotion?
- What are the elements involved in the promotion?
- Who is responsible for marketing the event or promotion?
- How many staff members are needed to execute the event?
- What materials and supplies are needed for the event or promotion?
- Who is responsible for working with suppliers to obtain the materials and supplies?

■ What are the specific deadlines associated with the event or promotion, such as obtaining a mailing list, or printing and sending invitations?

■ What are some potential problems, and what are their solutions?

The most common problems are those affecting inventory, product quality, staffing, and storage. Planning at this level will help ensure the success of your event or promotion. Since your staff members are an integral part of your product and your promotions, they should fully understand the plan before it is implemented.

Activity

La Cucina's Promotion Mix

Nancy Greco moved to Park City, Utah, with her husband about three years ago and has been running her restaurant, La Cucina, for the past two years. La Cucina is a casual restaurant offering a full menu of traditional, moderately priced Italian cuisine.

In the year before the restaurant opened, while Nancy was developing her restaurant concept and business plan, she was somewhat out of touch with the local community. Being a newcomer to Park City, which has a population of approximately 120,000 people, and having a busy schedule has not given Nancy the time to network within the city.

In the last three months, sales have been suffering, and other casual Italian restaurants have been opening within her market area. To confront this, Nancy is looking closely at the public relations area of her promotion mix. Keeping in mind the enormous amount of time and effort it took to plan and open La Cucina, Nancy is fully aware that she also needs to get involved in her community.

In two weeks, the annual Park City Fair, highlighting the best of the city, will be held at Willow Wood Park. This fair offers concessions, amusement rides, games, and a keynote speaker. The fair is the annual highlight of the city, and almost every business is represented in some fashion. But what is really drawing Nancy's attention to this fair is that the local newspaper is showcasing the "best family restaurants in Park City." Nancy quickly signs up for the event and rents a space to display her menu, offer samples, and give out discount coupons. She is also coming prepared with her signature lasagna dish for the reporter to try.

1 Nancy is receiving free publicity, but is there anything she should be concerned about? Explain why or why not.

_____

_____

_____

_____

_____

_____

2 What other activities could Nancy have done to make sure she succeeded in the public relations portion of her promotion mix?

_____

_____

_____

3 What other suggestions would you have for Nancy for this particular event and future events?

_____

_____

_____

4 Looking at the entire promotion mix, how can Nancy use each component at this particular fair?

A Advertising:

_____

_____

B Public relations:

_____

_____

C Sales promotions:

_____

_____

D Personal selling:

_____

_____

Preparing Your Staff

In many instances, your staff is the best sales force. Knowledgeable servers should be able to explain current promotions to guests who are unaware of them. Keeping your staff not only trained but also motivated will help ensure the success of your promotion.

Before a promotion takes place, ensure that your staff knows the promotion details and trained on how to implement the promotion. If your promotion includes a new menu item, also make sure that staff members know the item's ingredients, especially potential allergens, and its nutritional features. In addition, if a promotion might increase the number of guests over a certain period, ensure that staff are scheduled accordingly.

Tracking the Promotion

Once you have implemented a promotion, you should monitor it to ensure that things are going the way you planned and there are no problems to be addressed. The implementation checklist you developed during the planning stage will help you to monitor the early part of the promotion. In addition, you should constantly track sales, inventory, staffing, and other aspects to make sure the promotion is being implemented correctly and is having the forecasted effect on business. To monitor a promotion, follow these guidelines:

- Meet regularly with your promotion team and employees to give and receive updates on the promotion results.

- Regularly communicate with your suppliers to update them on your restaurant's changing needs and to ensure that they can accommodate you.

- Track sales and other relevant measures before, during, and after the promotion.

The sales numbers provide the foundation for evaluating whether the promotion was effective and provided a good return on investment. After the promotion has been implemented and run its course, the evaluation stage allows the restaurant to determine the promotion's success. (This evaluation is discussed in Chapter 6.)

Summary

Promotions provide many benefits. They attract customers, increase business in general and specific ways, introduce or highlight menu items, help you compete, encourage customers to buy more, and reinforce or define your restaurant's image.

The promotion mix is a business's entire marketing communications program. It is critical to the success of both new and established restaurants. The promotion mix consists of four parts: advertising, public relations, sales promotions, and personal selling.

To get the best return on your investment in promotions and to ensure your promotions are successful, create a promotion plan that defines your promotion mix and how to implement it. The promotion mix should support your restaurant's marketing plan and objectives, and the components of the promotion mix should adequately support each other. The promotion mix also should convey an appropriate image for your operation.

The first step in planning your promotion mix is identifying your target audience. The next step is to begin developing your communication strategies and objectives. This part of the process involves assessing what customers already know, considering your product life cycle, designing a schedule for the plan, setting objectives and measurements, and determining the message you want to communicate. All of these actions should support your restaurant's marketing plan.

After developing strategies and objectives, select the components of your promotion mix and choose the tactics that best support your promotional strategy. If you are planning to use advertising, choose the appropriate media for your marketing communications. Your choice should depend on the media type best suited for conveying your message and the reach of individual media vehicles. Also, develop a scheduling strategy before you purchase advertising.

You also need to choose media vehicles for your public relations activities. Public relations involves creating relationships with the community and the media. Both these relationships are necessary to generate positive publicity.

If you are using sales promotions, you must choose the types of promotions that best support your marketing plan. Sales promotions need to support your marketing plan, your product positioning, and your restaurant's image. Therefore, carefully consider your choices in sales promotion methods and materials.

Since your staff interacts with customers for every purchase, your promotion mix should also include personal selling. To ensure your servers do a good job in this area, you need to keep them informed of your promotions and train them in sales techniques. Designated sales staff also may be involved in personal selling for specific areas, such as banquet or catering services.

Cooperative marketing activities can increase your promotions' return on investment. Typically, cooperative marketing involves sales promotions and advertising. A related practice is the use of trade-outs or bartering.

To successfully implement your promotion plan, use a checklist to stay organized. Use the checklist to identify who is doing what and when and also to consider various situations that can affect the plan's implementation. Make time to fully prepare your staff for an event or promotion.

As part of tracking a promotion after you implement it, talk regularly with staff members and suppliers. Monitor sales and other measures before, during, and after the promotion to provide a foundation for evaluating the promotion's success.

Review Your Learning

1 List at least three benefits of promotions.

_____

_____

_____

_____

_____

2 List three benefits of public relations.

_____

_____

_____

_____

_____

3 Which are examples of sales promotions?

A. Press releases, press kits, Web sites

B. Coupons, contests, free samples

C. Newspapers, television, radio

D. Upselling, suggestive selling, networking

4 What are the main steps in developing a promotional plan?

A. Choose the promotion mix, identify media, choose promotions, and implement the plan

B. Develop the marketing plan, identify the target market, and determine measurements

C. Identify the target audience, develop strategies and objectives, and determine tactics

D. Brainstorm ideas, research the market environment, and create a checklist

5 What are the components of the promotion mix?

A. Special pricing, frequent shopper programs, premiums, special events

B. Personal selling, public relations, sales promotions, and advertising

C. Promotions, product, place (distribution), and price

D. Target audience, promotional strategies, plan objectives, promotional tactics

6 Which are examples of personal selling?

A. Press releases, press kits, Web sites

B. Coupons, restaurant tours, deals

C. Newspapers, television, radio

D. Upselling, suggestive selling, networking

7 Which areas are most likely to cause problems when implementing a promotion plan?

A. Inventory, staffing, product quality

B. Customer response, publicity, target audience

C. Sanitation, budget strategy, employee benefits

D. Ambience, décor, restaurant concept

8 Why should employees be trained as part of a promotion plan?

A. To ensure good customer service, ensure the promotion is implemented properly, and motivate employees

B. To make sure staff can give customers information about ingredients and persuade new customers to patronize your restaurant

C. To verify staffing is adequate, track the promotion, and evaluate employee performance

D. To fulfill sanitation regulations, make sure employees know their jobs, and guarantee product quality

Evaluation and ROI

6

Inside This Chapter
- Evaluating the Marketing Plan
- Evaluating External Elements
- Evaluating Operational Internals
- Evaluating Return on Investment

After completing this chapter, you should be able to:
- Explain how to evaluate marketing plan success.
- Explain how to evaluate promotions.
- Explain how to evaluate product quality.
- Explain how to evaluate services.
- Explain how to do a menu sales analysis.
- List the areas that should be covered in the evaluation of a restaurant or foodservice operation, both externals and internals.
- Calculate return on investment in three ways: payback period, payback ratio, and ROI.

Test Your Knowledge

1 **True or False:** The three areas of a restaurant or foodservice operation that should be evaluated are menu items, services provided, and the price competitiveness of both. *(See p. 153.)*

2 **True or False:** Assessing which products are selling well and which are not is called a menu sales analysis. *(See p. 149.)*

3 **True or False:** It is important to evaluate subjective dimensions as well as objective dimensions of an operation. *(See p. 150.)*

4 **True or False:** A gap analysis is designed to assess your restaurant s performance against a standard. *(See p. 148.)*

5 **True or False:** Training is a sure way to increase productivity. *(See p. 159.)*

Key Terms

External factors

Gap analysis

Internal factors

Mise en place

Standard operating procedures (SOPs)

Introduction

Your marketing plan is your best attempt at planning how to attract customers from your target market, how to please those customers with products and services, and how to deliver these products and services in a consistent and profitable way. This marketing plan might be a single set of actions, or it might have several subplans. Whichever case, you should evaluate your successes and failures at the end of the plan or each subplan. This chapter is about performing such evaluations.

First, you should evaluate the success of your marketing plan. There are internal and external factors that contribute to the success of this plan. You should look at these so you know why things worked out the way they did and what to do differently next time.

Then, whatever the outcome of this evaluation, you also should evaluate the different elements of your operation so you know which need improving to support your marketing plan and which are working satisfactorily.

After you have evaluated your operation, you will know how successful your past investments were and where to invest in the future. You also will know what non-investment aspects should be

How does the adage "It takes money to make money" relate to restaurant and foodservice operations?

improved to result in more benefits to you, to employees, and to customers. You must invest in your business to get it started and to make it grow and generate additional revenue. The question is not whether or not to invest, the question is:

- How much to invest

- In what areas to invest

- What benefits you will receive from your investment

You evaluations will answer these questions and allow you to better design your next marketing and operations plans.

Evaluating the Marketing Plan

Evaluation should begin as soon as the deadline date for the marketing plan has passed. Following are some points to remember if a goal was met:

- What in particular helped to achieve the goal?

- Were there any **internal factors**—elements the restaurant can control and improve—that contributed to the success?
  For example:

  ☐ Knowledgeable staff

  ☐ Great-tasting products at the right price

  ☐ New menu items

  ☐ Excellent service

- Were there any **external factors**—elements outside the operation that cannot be controlled—that contributed to the success?
  For example:

  ☐ Good economy

  ☐ Successful local events

  ☐ Results of local elections

  ☐ Improved or resolved national situation

  ☐ Increased interest in sporting events

  ☐ Increased interest in community-related activities

  ☐ Holidays, celebrations, or seasonal factors

Here are some points to consider if a goal was not met:

- What was the primary reason why the goal was not met?

■ Where there any internal factors that contributed to not meeting the goal? For example:

☐ Improper food preparation, especially for a new, unfamiliar item

☐ Excessive delay between food preparation and serving

☐ Untrained staff

☐ Unmotivated staff

☐ Wrong products served

☐ Products priced incorrectly

☐ Poor customer service

☐ Ineffective promotion strategy or implementation

☐ Shortage or absence of supplies

☐ Faulty or out-of-service equipment

■ Were there any external factors that contributed to not meeting the goal? For example:

☐ Depressed economy

☐ Major local layoff

☐ Severe weather; e.g., heat wave, rainstorm, slippery roads

☐ Natural disasters; e.g., hurricanes, floods

☐ Threats to public safety; e.g., terrorism, crime wave

Benefiting from the Evaluation

Once the evaluation phase is completed, it is important to use the information obtained to identify how to improve the success of your business. If you fell short of your goal of increasing guest checks, you will need to determine the cause, and then decide what you can do about it. For example, after the evaluation of a menu-item promotion, you realize that your staff did not upsell menu items as requested. There may be many reasons why your operation did not meet its goals. For example:

■ **The servers had never tried any of the menu items.** (See *Exhibit 6a.*) Thus, your servers felt uncomfortable selling items they did not know. One way to improve this situation is a two-phase training program for your servers. The first phase is to have your servers work with the chef when deciding which items are being promoted and having the servers taste each product so they become familiar with them. The second phase is to work with your servers on selling techniques that will increase sales of the products.

Exhibit 6a

Waitstaff should taste the menu items being promoted so they can give a personal recommendation.

■ **The menu items were not prepared, held, plated, and served as well as they should have been.** In this case, the solution might be improved training of the kitchen staff that includes a description of the menu items, their preparation, their shelf life, the labor requirements for their preparation, and the look of the plate presentations.

■ **The menu items were not explained clearly.** As a result, customers ended up believing that they contained unpopular ingredients or allergens. In this case, more nutritional information might be provided on the menu or on table tents.

■ **The length of the promotion was not understood by staff or customers.** As a result, food items were not available when customers thought they should be. The solution would be to improve communication of the promotion, so staff and customers clearly understand the beginning and ending dates of the promotion.

■ **You did not correctly estimate how difficult the promoted items were to prepare, how long they took to prepare, or how many employees were required to create them.** This caused excessive delay between the items being ordered and served. In this case, you must improve your estimation skills and even involve more people in this process so the estimates will be more accurate.

There are many reasons why things go wrong, and many reasons why they go right. You should evaluate what happened and determine how to fix the things that went wrong or how to repeat the things that went right. That is how you improve your operation.

You can separate the elements to be evaluated into two categories: external, or those things evident to customers, and internal, or the behind-the-scenes factors. Specifically, you must look at how well your operation does the following:

■ External elements

    ☐ Promotions

    ☐ Sales

    ☐ Products

    ☐ Service quality and value

    ☐ Service promptness

■ Internal elements

    ☐ Product quality control

    ☐ Preparation processes

    ☐ Cleanliness and sanitation

    ☐ Shelf life of supplies

    ☐ Service staff

You should also evaluate your overall measure of success: return on investment.

Evaluating External Elements

The external elements of your operation are those things that your customers experience directly. Their evaluation of these elements forms their sense of brand and value for your operation. Your goal in evaluating the external elements is to see things through the eyes of your customers so you will be better able to meet the needs of your target markets.

Evaluating Promotions

Accepting the status quo should never be done in any business, especially the restaurant business. Even when things are going well, you should always strive to do better. How can you tell how well your promotions are doing? This is when goals and evaluation come into play.

For example, you may have wanted to sell more pasta because it is a very profitable item to sell. Prior to the promotion, you should have set a specific goal, such as "By December 31, 2008, we will increase our sales of pasta dishes by $48,000, a 20 percent increase over last year."

When you have a goal, you can perform a **gap analysis**—a determination of the difference between your actual performance and your goal or a standard. (See *Exhibit 6b*.) The objective of a gap analysis is to determine where you are (and why) so you can close the gap as much as possible. Suppose that, with one month left to meet your goal, your restaurant has increased the sales of pasta dishes by only $40,000. As a restaurant manager, you want to close the gap between actual sales and your sales goal.

Prior to launching any promotion, you should develop a system to track the progress of the promotion. Areas to track include:

- **Sales of the promotional item**—The up-to-date actual sales of the promotional item should be calculated.

- **Amount sold after the promotion**—This is an important figure to identify. If you find that sales continue to climb after the promotion, then people are buying the item for its quality and not only because of the promotion.

- **Increased or decreased sales for other menu items during the same period**—This is called secondary sales. When a person dines at your restaurant because of the promotion and then buys another item, such as a glass of wine, a cocktail, or an appetizer, a secondary sale has occurred.

- **Number of new customers attained during the promotion**—This is basically tracking the number of new customers that

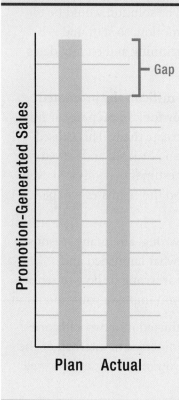

Exhibit 6b

Gap Analysis

Promotion-Generated Sales

Gap

Plan   Actual

dined in your restaurant specifically because of the promotion. This will have a long-term effect on your sales if these customers develop into long-term, repeat customers.

■ **Which server sold the most promotional menu items—** This identifies which server sold the most items during the promotional period. This information can be useful when evaluating performance. It is also helpful in determining what training needs to be conducted for servers who did not sell as much.

Communicating the results of the promotion to your service and kitchen employees is important for a variety of reasons:

■ Generates good feelings among staff members about their hard work

■ Builds teamwork and morale

■ Encourages ideas on how to improve performance

■ Fosters communication between front- and back-of-the-house employees

Exhibit 6c

Entrée Sales Analysis for Jack's Restaurant

Menu Item	Orders Sold	Menu Price	Sales	Margin per Order	Total Profit
Pot Roast	500	$11.00	$ 5,500	$ 2.63	$ 1,315
Meat Loaf	300	8.00	2,400	3.35	1,005
Chicken	500	9.00	4,500	2.81	1,405
Pork Chops	400	10.00	4,000	2.36	944
Whitefish	400	12.50	5,000	2.04	816
Lasagna	120	9.00	1,080	3.10	372

Evaluating Sales

In the restaurant business, your menu items are your products. To assess which products are selling well and which are not, you need to conduct a menu sales analysis. The outcome of this type of analysis will usually determine whether a menu item should be discontinued, moved on the menu, improved, or featured in a promotion. For example, Jack's Restaurant offers six dinner entrée items: pot roast, meat loaf, chicken, pork chops, whitefish, and lasagna. Jack conducts a menu sales analysis for a one-week period, as shown in *Exhibit 6c*. After reviewing the results, Jack sees that the two most profitable items (meat loaf and lasagna) are not selling as frequently as the others. Jack knows that the customers expect to see these items on the menu, so he cannot discontinue them. After reviewing customer comment cards, Jack realizes that some customers think the meat loaf has too much pepper and the lasagna does not have enough tomato sauce. Consequently, the chef improves both products by reducing

Exhibit 6d

Sample Menu-Item Quality and Variety Survey

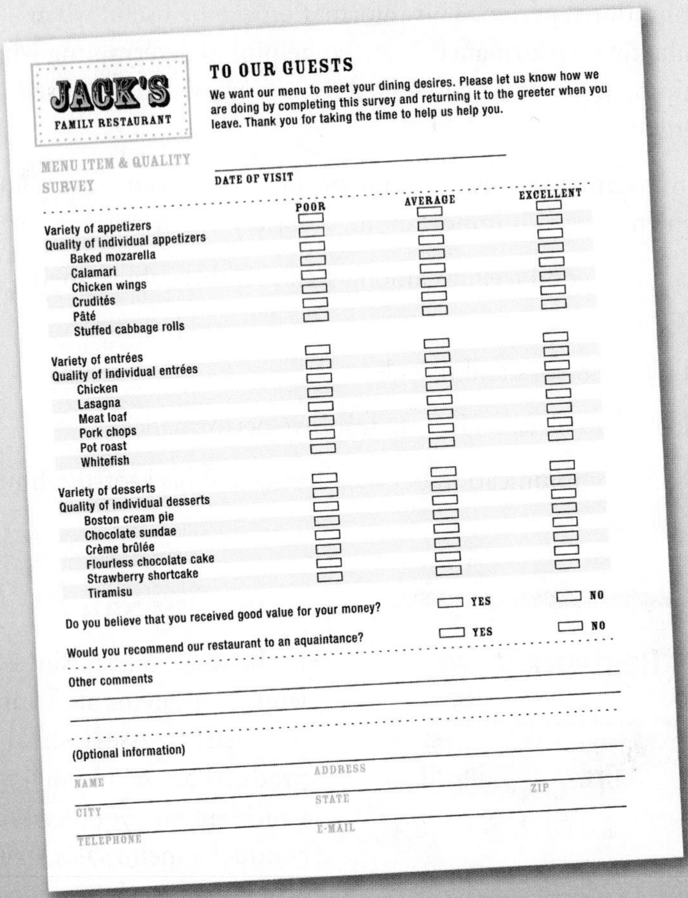

the pepper on the meat loaf and increasing the tomato sauce on the lasagna. Then Jack introduces the "new and improved" products through a sales promotion.

Evaluating Customer Satisfaction with Products

In addition to evaluating how well products sell, there are other aspects of your menu to evaluate: quality and variety. These factors are your customers' subjective opinions, so a customer survey is needed to measure them. The most common way of gathering customer opinions in a restaurant or foodservice operation is the comment card or survey. *Exhibit 6d* shows a typical menu-item survey. The results from your surveys or comment cards will give you valuable information about what the customers think about your menu items.

Evaluating Customer Satisfaction with Service Quality

As part of setting prices, you should check the prices your competitors charge and the services they offer. *Exhibit 6e* shows an example of such a comparison and the changes you made to bring your services into line with those of your competitors. Once your products and services are in line with those of your competitors, you can then evaluate the services you offer and how much your customers value these services.

For example, suppose you conduct a survey about the value of the services received, as shown in *Exhibit 6f*. The survey is handed to customers as the check is presented. The waitstaff asks the customers to complete the survey and return it to the greeter on their way out.

Exhibit 6e

Competitive Analysis of Services

Restaurant	Valet parking	Parking lot	Coat check	Doggie bags	Cloth linens	Family-style	Private room	Wine steward	Service style
Branson Chophouse	Free	No	$2.00	Yes	Yes	No	$50	No	English
Will's Steakhouse	$5.00	No	No	Yes	Yes	Yes	No	No	American
Carriage House	$8.00	Small	Free	Yes	Yes	No	Free	Yes	English
The Lantern	$6.00	Large	No	Yes	Yes	Yes	$75	No	American
The Coventry	Free	Large	Free	Yes	Yes	No	Free	Yes	English
Your Steakhouse	Added $5.00	Small	Free	Yes	Added	Yes	Lowered to $50	No	American

Exhibit 6f

Sample Service-Quality Survey

JACK'S FAMILY RESTAURANT

TO OUR GUESTS
We want your dining experience to be all that you hoped it would be. Please let us know how we are doing in meeting your service needs by completing this survey and returning it to the host when you leave. Thank you.

SERVICE - QUALITY SURVEY

DATE OF VISIT

	POOR	AVERAGE	EXCELLENT
Parking lot convenience			
Parking lot cleanliness			
Valet service value for price			
Friendliness of greeter/host			
Coat check service			
Décor			
Table location			
Linens and silverware			
Helpfulness of server			
Friendliness of server			
Accuracy of meal served			
Promptness of table service			
Cleanliness of restrooms			
Cleanliness of restaurant			
Quality of private room (if utilized)			

Do you believe that you received good value for your money? ☐ YES ☐ NO

Is there a particular employee you would like to single out for praise? ☐ YES ☐ NO
If yes, please explain.

Would you recommend our restaurant to an aquaintance? ☐ YES ☐ NO

Other comments

Analysis of such survey returns enables you to determine whether any changes are necessary. You should pay particular attention to the question about the customer receiving good value for the money. The answers to this question can help you evaluate how your customers feel your prices compare to the value of the services received. If customers believe that their money is well spent, it also means they value the services your operation offers. If any changes are needed, you can tell from the survey returns.

When analyzing comment cards and surveys, keep in mind that it is more common for people to complete them if they have had a poor experience than if they had a good experience.

151

Exhibit 6g

Voluntary Comments

Customer Opinion of Product or Service	Likelihood of Voluntary Comments
Outstanding	Sometimes
Excellent	
Very Good	Rarely
Average	
Poor	
Bad	Often
Awful	

Voluntary feedback has a bias toward the negative.

Exhibit 6h

Signs of Service Promptness Problems

■ If the customer is sitting and doing nothing, or looking for the server, the customer wants some service. The service could be to have something corrected or could be serving the next course.

■ If the customer is finished with the current course and is sitting for a while, the customer probably wants speedier service. A quick question by the server will verify this.

■ If the customer lets the course sit for a while or is not finished with one course when the next course is served, service is too speedy.

If the negative comments are random, it may simply indicate a one-time bad experience. (See *Exhibit 6g.*) However, you should still investigate a negative comment and respond to the guest. Negative comments that are consistent or follow a pattern indicate a more serious problem.

Evaluating Customer Satisfaction with Service Promptness

No one likes to waste time, and no one likes to have other people waste his or her time. Promptness is a valued characteristic of good service. However, the customer, not the server, defines promptness. What is "prompt" service for one customer might be "rushed" service for another customer and "slow" service for a third. This means that servers must be able to read their customers and determine how quickly they want to be served. (See *Exhibit 6h.*)

As a manager, you should constantly be monitoring the promptness of service provided by your service staff. All you have to do is look for the same signs that the servers should be looking for. Going a step further is even better: talk to your customers about the promptness of service and whether it is meeting their needs.

If promptness of service is a problem, two things need to be done:

■ Alert the service staff that promptness is important and that the customer sets the standard.

■ Train the service staff in detecting the speed of service desired by a customer.

Evaluating Operational Internals

The external elements of your operation are generated by the workings of internal factors. These internal factors must be evaluated to find out what is going on and to determine what needs to be improved.

Evaluating your operation's internals is much like an annual checkup. To conduct such an evaluation, you must have standards against which to evaluate actual performance. Procedural standards are called **standard operating procedures (SOPs),** and they should be documented. SOPs are overall guidelines that employees of the restaurant must follow.

The internal factors that should be evaluated include:

- Product quality
- Meal preparation procedures
- Cleanliness and sanitation
- Shelf life of supplies
- Service staff
- Training
- Customer service standards
- Menu item characteristics

Exhibit 6i

The taste and appearance of every menu item must be up to quality standards.

Evaluating Product Quality Control

Your menu items, for the most part, are your restaurant in the eyes of your customers. Your customers are continually evaluating your menu items, and this evaluation is the primary reason why (or why not) customers will return to your restaurant. You should not wait for business to fall off before you discover that the quality of your menu items has declined. Evaluating your menu items is the responsibility of everyone in your operation—chefs, servers, managers, and owners—and should be done regularly. (See *Exhibit 6i.*) This is the only way to ensure that product standards are being met and that menu items taste they way they should.

In planning your operation (see Chapter 3), you should have established standards for the taste and appearance of your menu items. Obviously, these standards are useless unless your employees adhere to them. As a manager of a restaurant or foodservice operation, you must set up and continuously operate a quality inspection system to verify this.

Several things you can do include:

- Checking each plate as it comes from the kitchen on its way to your customers

- Randomly taste-testing menu items, making sure to sample every menu item each month

- Using a "secret shopper" who visits your operation anonymously, orders and samples a complete meal, and then gives you detailed feedback on its taste and appearance, as well as the quality of service

Evaluating Preparation Processes

Your operation might serve great dishes that people love and are willing to pay for, but if your labor costs are too high, you could be in trouble. On a continuing basis, you must evaluate how difficult it is to prepare each item, how long it takes to prepare each item, and how many employees are required to prepare each item. All these dimensions of food preparation have costs that must be paid for by revenue, and the higher these costs are, the lower your profit. There are two ways to determine these costs, and both have advantages and disadvantages:

Exhibit 6j

Your food preparation procedures must have quality standards, and you must ensure that the taste and appearance of every menu item is up to the standards.

- **Observing preparation in action.** You can observe your kitchen employees as they prepare actual customer orders (see *Exhibit 6j*) and as they do the *mise en place*—preorder preparation work. The advantage of this method is that you can see how people actually do things. The disadvantages are that it takes a large amount of time and the rush of meal hours affects how things are done.

- **Running preparation tests.** You can run test preparations of menu items during off hours. The advantage of this method is that you can determine the ideal preparation time. The disadvantage is that employees will know they are being tested and will make sure they follow all the required procedures, even the ones they might skip in their actual work.

The ideal solution is to use a combination of both methods.

Evaluating Cleanliness and Sanitation

Maintaining a clean establishment is not only important for proper handling of food, but also for increasing sales. Restaurant professionals realize that their customers expect a clean and safe place to eat. Keeping the establishment clean reduces the chances of slips, trips, and falls by employees and customers; it also reduces or prevents outbreaks of foodborne illness.

Your local health department has established sanitation standards that you must meet in order to be certified to conduct business. It establishes procedures in these areas to ensure that your guests and employees are safe from problems concerning general safety and food safety.

In turn, you must establish procedures and standards for cleaning. Since there are so many areas to clean in a restaurant, you must be well-organized. One way to do this is to develop a cleaning schedule for your operation. This cleaning schedule should indicate:

- What needs to be cleaned
- When it needs to be cleaned
- How it should be cleaned
- Who should do the cleaning

An example of a cleaning schedule is shown in *Exhibit 6k*.

Exhibit 6k

Restaurant Cleaning Schedule

Item	What	When	Use	Who
Floors	■ Wipe up spills	■ Immediately	■ Cloth mop and bucket, broom and dustpan	Bussers
	■ Damp mop	■ Once per shift, between rushes	■ Mop, bucket, safety signs	
	■ Scrub	■ Daily, at closing	■ Brushes, squeegee, bucket, detergent, safety signs	
	■ Strip, reseal	■ Every six months	■ Check written procedures	
Walls and ceilings	■ Wipe up splashes	■ As soon as possible	■ Clean cloth, detergent	Dish-washing staff
	■ Wash walls	■ Food-prep and cooking areas: daily		
		■ All other areas: first of the month		
Worktables	■ Clean and sanitize tops	■ Between uses and at the end of the day	■ See cleaning procedure for each table	Prep cooks
	■ Empty, clean, and sanitize drawers	■ Weekly	■ See cleaning procedure for table	

155

Developing a cleaning schedule is not enough. As a manager, you also must monitor the cleaning process while it is taking place, and afterward verify that everything has been cleaned according to your maintenance schedule and cleanliness standards. This means that you or an employee must conduct regular inspections of all the cleaned areas, and these inspections must be part of the cleaning schedule.

Evaluating Shelf Life of Supplies

Another kind of food safety involves the shelf life of food supplies. These materials deteriorate under the best of storage conditions. First, you must set standards for the storage of the different types of food supplies. Second, you must monitor their storage to ensure that the standards are being followed. Third, you must understand and follow expiration dates and shelf-life guidelines to determine how long food supplies are safe to use. When food items exceed their shelf life or their expiration date, they cannot be sold or served. Your local health department has information that you can use to train your staff about shelf-life guidelines.

Exhibit 6l

The service staff is your "face" to the customer. The quality of your staff's service is a major factor in your success.

Evaluating Service Staff

Your service staff members are the salespeople for your restaurant. They are responsible for ensuring that your customers receive what they want and for suggesting items that customers may want. (See *Exhibit 6l.*) It is imperative for your service staff to provide good customer service through their knowledge of the menu items sold and to meet your customers' expectations.

Are Staff Knowledgeable and Credible?

The service staff must know what is going on in the kitchen. They need to know what items are offered, how they are made, and how they taste. For this to happen, they need to communicate with the chef or other kitchen personnel before each shift to review what items are being prepared for that day, what the specials are, and how all these items are prepared. By understanding the products offered, the service staff will be able to answer customers' questions.

It is important that service staff have credibility in the eyes of customers. One sure way to lose credibility is an inability to describe the menu items. Many customers ask the service staff to recommend an item, which means that the service staff should taste a product before recommending it. When your service staff recommends an item they have not tasted, it will usually be the highest-priced item, which may offend a customer. So taste-testing all menu items is critical for employees who serve guests. A good manager ensures that the staff tastes the products and also identifies what to look for in a product. For example, if a guest cannot eat spicy food, the server must be able to recommend the appropriate menu items.

Do Staff Provide Friendly and Helpful Service?

The restaurant and foodservice industry is a service business. Customers expect to be served by friendly, helpful people. It is every employee's job to ensure that customers' expectations are met night after night. An important skill that a server should possess is the ability to read a guest's feelings about the level of service. For example, if a couple comes in for dinner and plans to attend a show that same evening, service should be quick. However, if a couple is celebrating their wedding anniversary at your restaurant, then service should be slower paced.

As a result of evaluating your externals and internals, you should have a good idea of what to improve to make your establishment, products, and services more attractive to your target market. Some improvements are merely changes in procedures that require a little training; other improvements require much larger investments in effort, time, and money. These latter improvements should be evaluated for their return on investment, as you learned in Chapter 3. Now is the time to make such evaluations.

Evaluating Return on Investment

When you make plans for your operation, you should set financial goals such as payback period, payback ratio, and return on investment. (*See Exhibit 6m.*) For example, if you decide to buy a new grill for your kitchen, you should identify exactly what benefits it would bring to your operation.

Exhibit 6m

Formulas for Evaluating Return on Investment

Payback period—Length of time it takes for an investment to pay for itself

Dollars invested ÷ Dollar return per year = Payback period in years

Payback ratio—Ratio of money returned over the life of the investment to the amount of the investment

Lifetime dollars returned ÷ Dollars invested = Payback ratio

Return on investment—Payback ratio expressed as a percentage

Lifetime dollars returned ÷ Dollars invested × 100% = ROI

Evaluating Returns with Hard Data

In Chapter 3, you considered investing in a grill—the investment looked like a good one, based on the figures that were used. Determining the savings or additional revenue obtained from investing in equipment such as a new grill involves placing the actual numbers into the formulas identified in *Exhibit 6m.* When you compare the actual results to the planned results, you will know how well the investment paid off.

To achieve the estimated return on investment for an item such as a grill, the item needs to provide the actual return estimated for each year of its lifetime, and the item needs to last as long as its expected lifetime. Unfortunately, there are many reasons why this may not happen, such as:

- The yearly returns were overestimated.

- The item cannot be used as originally predicted.

- The item requires repair, which reduces the annual returns.

- The item does not last for the expected lifetime.

- The item is replaced with newer technology before its useful life has been reached.

As a manager, you have to determine whether you got enough return despite these limiting factors.

Evaluating Returns with Soft Data

For investments in which the returns are only subjective estimates, such as the return on a new music system, actual numbers are difficult to come by and inaccurate. As a result, the calculations for return are not as accurate or useful as they are with purely monetary investments like bonds and savings accounts. In these cases, you have to rely on your "gut feeling" or your own subjective evaluation. Nevertheless, some evaluation of investments with subjective elements should be done so you can make decisions about whether to keep them, remove them, or improve them.

Evaluating Return on a Training Investment

The returns on an investment depend on the actual use of the investment over the number of years that the investment is supposed to bring returns. An investment such as training has the expectation that the trained employees will actually use the skills and knowledge they have gained for a long period of time. Unfortunately, there are many reasons why this might not happen:

- The supervisor "untrains" the employees back to the old ways.

- The employees leave the operation.

- The employees get too little reward for implementing the training and stop doing it the new way.

You can see that it is not enough to do a good job of planning your investments; you also have to monitor and manage them throughout their lifetimes so they actually achieve their predicted returns. This means you must do regular evaluations of your operations. Additionally, remember that when your operations are working properly, you will have a better chance of successfully implementing your marketing plan and, ultimately, increasing your profit.

Think About It...

More than one out of four table-service operators increased the portion of their budget allocated for training in 2006. Why?

Source: National Restaurant Association

Activity

Analyzing What Really Happened

You are the manager of Pete's Pizza and Pasta. Recently, you set up an aggressive plan to increase sales and your customer base. You succeeded in increasing return visits by your current customers. However, you fell considerably short at increasing the number of new customers and increasing the average guest check.

Shown below is your business plan for the year and your actual results. Explain why you did not meet your new customer and guest check goals. Then list the areas that you should concentrate on improving for the coming year in order to do better.

Business Plan for Pete's Pizza and Pasta

Overall Objective:

Pete's Pizza and Pasta will increase sales by a minimum of $100,000 over sales of the last fiscal year. We will increase sales by adding new customers, increasing the frequency of visits, and increasing sales per guest check.

New Customers:

We will add 500 customers to our existing customer base of 4,000 over the fiscal year.

Action Plan:

- Develop a referral plan with other businesses in the area.
- Conduct a direct mail campaign.
- Introduce new desserts.
- Add entertainment on weekend nights.
- Advertise quarterly in local papers.

Repeat Customers:

We will have 50 percent of our customers return to our store three times a year, up from two times a year for the previous year. The percent of returning customers also will increase 25 percent from last year.

Action Plan:

- Develop a direct mail list and calendar to communicate with our customers.
- Provide activities every three months to encourage our customers to come back.
- Establish a frequent dining program with a discount on the fourth visit.

Increase the Guest Check:

Increase sales from $11.00 per guest to $13.75. This is a 25 percent increase.

Action Plan:

- Raise prices on every item by 10 percent.
- Suggestive-sell bigger-sized pizzas and drinks.
- Introduce a new dessert tray to customers.

Sales Goals		
New Customers	**Last Year's Actual**	**This Year's Goal**
Number of new customers	300	500
Average guest check	$ 11.00	$ 13.75
Sales from new customers (Number × Average check)	3,300.00	6,875.00
If customers return two times a year (2 × Sales)	6,600.00	13,750.00
If customers return three times a year (3 × Sales)		20,625.00
Sales from new customers (actual and goal sales)	6,600.00	20,625.00
Increased sales from new customers (This year's goal − Last year's actual)		14,025.00
Repeat Customers	**Last Year's Actual**	**This Year's Goal**
Number of repeat customers	1,000	2,000
Average guest check	$ 11.00	$ 13.75
Sales from repeat customers (Number × Average check)	11,000.00	27,500.00
If customers return two times a year (2 × Sales)	22,000.00	55,000.00
If customers return three times a year (3 × Sales)		82,500.00
Sales from repeat customers (Actual and goal sales)	22,000.00	82,500.00
Increased sales from repeat customers (This year's goal − Last year's actual)		60,500.00

Projections

Overall sales projected (New customer goal + Repeat customer goal): $103,125
Increased sales (New customer increase + Repeat customer increase): $74,525

Results One Year Later		
Customers	**Goal**	**Actual**
Number of new customers	500	300
Number of return visits by new customers	3 times	2 times
Number of repeat customers	2,000	2,000
Number of return visits by repeat customers	3 times	3 times
Average guest check	$13.75	$12.00

Give some reasons why you think Pete's Pizza and Pasta did not meet their new customer and guest check goals. Provide your thoughts as to what areas the restaurant should focus on.

Summary

Your marketing plan is your way of determining exactly how to attract, please, and retain customers and achieve your target profits. At the end of every marketing plan or marketing plan subpart, you should evaluate how well you did so you can benefit from your mistakes and successes alike. Typically, any gaps are due to uncontrollable external factors or controllable internal elements. You must take note of the uncontrollable external elements that helped or hindered your plan so you can correctly incorporate them into the next marketing plan. Likewise, you must determine what improvements are needed in your controllable internal elements so you can improve them as needed.

Establishing goals and standards are very important for increasing the profitability of your restaurant. Evaluating these goals to see what worked and what did not will help your operation become more effective. Proper evaluation will allow you to minimize making the same mistake over and over again. Conversely, evaluating successes will enable you to target your resources toward areas that will make the business strong.

Review Your Learning

1 Conducting a gap analysis is important when evaluating a promotion because it

A. identifies what you are doing wrong.

B. assesses your actual results against a goal or standard.

C. identifies who is not performing effectively.

D. identifies why areas need to be improved.

2 The areas of your operation to evaluate include all of these *except*

A. your competitive advantage.

B. your return on investment.

C. your product quality.

D. the value of your services to your customers.

3 A menu analysis is implemented to assess

A. what your chef is good at making.

B. how well your menu communicates.

C. how your customers like the menu layout and readability.

D. which menu items are selling and which ones are not.

4 Standard operating procedures (SOPs) are important because they

A. state overall guidelines that a restaurant needs to follow.

B. assist management when an employee needs to be terminated.

C. are given to the Better Business Bureau to maintain your legal status.

D. enable you to qualify for investment funds.

5 When evaluating service quality, you should do any or all of the following *except*

A. compare your sales to competitors' sales with similar services.

B. gather the opinions of your service staff and dining room manager.

C. use a customer survey or comment cards.

D. observe your service staff in action during busy meal periods.

6 Your upselling training program cost $5,000 to implement. Now you notice that profit has increased by $20,000. What is your return on investment?

A. 400%   C. 25%

B. 4,000%   D. $5,000

7 To evaluate product quality, you might do all of these *except*

A. conduct procedural tests.

B. conduct taste tests.

C. evaluate product appearance.

D. use a secret shopper.

8 When evaluating the success of your marketing plan, you should do all of these *except*

A. determine whether the goal was met.

B. look at both internal and external factors.

C. analyze why the goal was not met.

D. figure out which employees failed so you can fire them.

Notes

Field Project

Advertising or Promotion Evaluation

This project will allow you to focus on the key marketing issues in this guide and to determine how the material presented is used in a real-world situation within a particular operation. You will prepare a detailed explanation of which marketing efforts in the operation you believe are working, as well as what you would suggest for changes or improvements.

The goal of this activity is not for you to directly match what you think the operation's goals should be versus what they actually are, but to further understand that every operation will actively choose what to incorporate into their establishment's promotions based on the market variables present.

The Assignment

Work with a restaurant in your area to gather the information listed below about the establishment:

1 Current menu

2 Information on the local area in which the restaurant is located

3 Advertising piece

4 Information on competition

5 Competitor's advertising piece or promotional item

6 Promotional item/piece

7 Organizational chart

8 Past financial statements (with marketing break outs)

9 Mission statement

10 Operation/employee schedule

There is no set number on the amount of items to include for your evaluation; however, the more information you include, the more thorough your analysis will be. Much of this information may be accessible over the Internet.

Once you have researched the operation, evaluate its advertising piece or promotion in light of the other information you have obtained, and prepare a report containing their evaluations and recommendations.

Here are some things you should include in your report:

1 Brief overview of the restaurant

☐ Classification of the restaurant in terms of service and style

☐ History of the restaurant (if available)

☐ Mission statement, (the restaurant's values)

☐ Current state of the establishment (look at financial and operations reports)

continued on next page

Advertising or Promotion Evaluation *continued from the previous page*

2 The restaurant's market

- ☐ Demographics
- ☐ Competitors

3 Advertising piece or promotional item

- ☐ What is the intended goal of the promotional item?
- ☐ How would you evaluate it?
- ☐ Does it target the correct market?
- ☐ Suggestions on making it better?
- ☐ Ideas/suggestions for additional pieces?
- ☐ Is the image supported by this piece?

4 Anticipated outcome of the advertising piece or promotional item

- ☐ Do you think this advertising or promotional will be a success?
- ☐ How will this impact sales/revenue?
- ☐ Do you believe this fulfilled the mission of ROI?
- ☐ How will this impact the long-term success of the hotel in general?

5 How the piece actually fared

Index